Corrective Lenses
A Rethinking of
American Punishment Systems

Daniel Throop and James Keown

Quail Valley Publishing, Inc.

Quail Valley Publishing
Holts Summit, MO 65043, USA

First edition: November 2014

ISBN 978-1-312-77401-8

Printed in the United States of America
www.quailvalleypublishing.com

Table of Contents

Foreword i

Introduction iii

The Island Effect: Social Marooning in
Corrections as Extra-Judicial Punishment 1-22
Daniel Throop

Capitalism and Ontological Otherness in
Modern Day America 23-48
Shaun

Mandatory Return: Determinate Sentencing
and Its Impact on Recidivism 49-74
James Keown

A Vicious Cycle: The Effect of Child
Abuse on Juvenile Arrest 75-104
Emily Henson

Unlocking the Potential 105-122
Steven Quinlan

Uncaptive Minds and Hearts: Boston University
Prison Education Program, Its Impact on
Student Rehabilitation 123-142
Silvia

The Act of Guilt: Performativity
in the Justice System 143-159
Jennifer Hernandez

Curating the Blues: Prison-Radio Correspondence
as an Act of Co-Creation 161-183
Kye

Prisons and Playacting; Reclaiming Agency and Identity
Through the Prison Arts Projects at MECC 185-205
Adam Vander Tuig

Overcoming Recidivism from A
Position of Inequality 207-230
Mark Brouillard

<u>Foreword</u>

As I have discovered during the compilation of this work, some moments are so special that they capture you more than you capture them. Dr. Kaia Stern's Sociology class was just such a moment, and this anthology is an attempt to commemorate the transformative experience which we all shared along with the originality of the ideas that it inspired. Hopefully, the kaleidoscopic vision of my classmates can serve as a powerful reminder that we blind ourselves when we fail to see the humanity in others. Sadly, it is this sort of monoculed superiority on the part of policymakers which has fueled the creation, and punishment, of a dehumanized criminal class in America today.

Vision can be deceptive, especially from the outside looking in, which is why I can't thank Kaia, Jacob, Amanda, Lauren, Emily, Silvia, Nicki, Jennifer, Shawn, Adam and Kye enough for boldly transcending the social boundaries between us. In so doing, you all became the termites of change which Kaia encourages us to be, and you affirmed your own humanity as much as you did ours. For that, you have earned our undying respect and gratitude. Anwar El-Sadat said that "He who cannot change the very fabric of his thought will never be able to change reality." I think it's clear that our collaboration has changed us all for the better, and through the corrective lenses of understanding, solutions to the social ills which plague American culture seem much less illusory.

Daniel S. Throop
October 2014

Introduction

There is a lot of talk these days about prison reform. A lot of talk. But very little action. It seems that many Americans understand that the current system is broken. One recent poll reported that nearly seven-in-ten believe the system is so dysfunctional that people leaving prison are actually more hardened than before they entered. In other words, America's ever-expanding network of prisons, in the opinion of those polled, is doing more harm than good to public safety.

Proposals from the right, the left, and everywhere in between are bandied about regularly. It seems that everyone from the local chamber of commerce to the PTA have an idea on how best to fix the problem. What's surprising is who is left out of the conversation -- the over two million men and women who are currently incarcerated in the United States. One might think they would have something to say about the conditions that led to their incarceration, and certainly some ideas about what will keep them from returning once released.

Any doctor, at least any who is worth their salt, will say that the best way to diagnose an illness is to start with a good patient history. And the best way to heal that patient is to positively engage them in the treatment process. The doctor-patient analogy, however, makes some very squeamish. Those in the crime is a choice camp push back against anything that gives the perception of mitigating the responsibility of those who have committed crimes. That said, it is fairly settled fact that scores of outside factors contribute to a person breaking the law, most notable poor economic conditions and lack of education. Unfortunately, answers to problems driven by these kinds of variables are hard. And they certainly don't fit into neat little sound bites that can be served up on the nightly news.

What follows is a series of selected essays that attempts to address some of the most pressing problems facing the American criminal justice system. These authors don't flirt around with the clean edges of the issues as many politicians and pundits do. Instead, each writer dives deep into one of the myriad of complicated topics that must be addressed if there is ever to be a successful and comprehensive reform of the system.

Yes, there have been many papers, articles, and books in recent years with a similar goal. What sets this book apart is that every author presented has spent time in prison. More specifically, each writer has spent time at MCI-Norfolk in Massachusetts. Some are serving time for a variety of crimes. Others were regular visitors to the facility.

Each author was a member of a unique class offered during the Spring 2014 semester of the Boston University Prison Education Program at MCI-Norfolk. The class was officially called, SO-501: Special study of ethics in race, crime, and punishment. Unofficially, it was called the Harvard Seminar. The class was comprised of ten men serving time and ten graduate students from Harvard. Guided by the course's professor, Dr. Kaia Stern, the students explored a wide range of topics related to crime and punishment. As a final project, each student selected one topic that resonated with them and crafted a research paper. Once done, it became clear that the class had not only captured fresh perspectives on current issues, but also identified many topics that are not even on most reformers' radars.

The walls and fences surrounding America's prisons are not just there to keep men and women in. They're also there to keep the general public out. That means those with the most knowledge on prison topics are those who are incarcerated and those who are able to venture past guard towers and into a world where standing counts, strip searches, and dehumanizing practices are commonplace. The following essays hope to offer a virtual access into this shrouded world. It should be noted, though, that none of these papers are the final words on any of the discussed subjects. Instead, they are conversation starters. Each idea has been diligently researched and thoroughly developed. But there is always more that can be said that must be said.

Robin Williams asked his students in the movie *The Dead Poets Society*, 'What will your verse be?" In the complex realm of criminal justice reform, here are the verses presented by some of the students of the 2014 BU PEP Harvard Seminar.

October 2014
James P. Keown

The Island Effect: Social Marooning in Corrections as Extra-Judicial Punishment

Daniel S. Throop

April 8, 2014

Abstract

Objectives: To examine the causal factors of social death within punitive structures of correctional isolation, and to assess the negative outcomes associated with such extra-judicially applied forms of punishment in the creation of collateral consequences. Method: Research is centered around class texts, sociological studies, and DOC correctional policies. Results: Findings affirm that the effects of correctional isolation destroy social networks and undermine successful reentry. Conclusion: The abuse of the state's power to punish via social isolation results in relational genocide.

 Keywords: Island Effect, Social Marooning, Extra-Judicial, Social Death, Collateral Consequences, and Relational Genocide.

Introduction

Upon the vast ocean of humanity, prison atolls dot the seascape like small slabs of stony hopelessness. Societal castaways who wash up on the shores of these islands of isolation are destined to experience a dark degree of desertion. The intense feelings of loneliness which ensue are the hallmarks of social marooning, whereby one realizes that no rescue ship is coming for them. Time and distance corrosively combine to erode all remaining remnants of external relationships to the point of a person's virtual non-existence to society, i.e. social death. Internal relationships amongst peers, staff, and volunteers are also targeted for destruction by correctional authorities as all forms of social contact and communication are severely regulated and often contrabanded. The overall reduction of interpersonal support systems through the removal of a prisoner's access to connective bridges of community are harbingers of the Island Effect, which reduces the friendly and familiar to the alien and alone.

The Massachusetts Department of Corrections (DOC) captains eighteen such islands with a total population of 11,149 human beings.[1] When one factors in all of the families and friendships which were once associated with such a large prison population, the sheer numbers of the socially dead amount to nothing less than state-sanctioned relational genocide (Relational genocide being the systematic extermination of a person's interpersonal relationships, cumulatively, via social starvation). Fueled by the mournful tears of the socially marooned, a tsunami of sadness sweeps across the archipelagoes of corrections until the personal identities of the incarcerated are reduced to mere flotsam. As Yale anthropologist Donald Braman asserts, "In this sense, the incarceration of an offender is not simply the sanctioning of an individual, but part of a broader corrosion of social bonds-bonds that sustain people, particularly people in difficult circumstances".[2]

It is the goal of this research to illuminate, more fully, the extent to which punitive forms of social isolation in correctional systems adversely impacts the physical, emotional, and psychological well being of the socially condemned, while also highlighting the collateral consequences which are created as a result of extra-judicial correctional policies. Existing scholarship fails to incorporate the full gamut of collateral consequences, especially regarding interpersonal and relational losses, which are extra-judicial in that they are arbitrarily accrued punishments meted out by correctional authorities, not the courts, at the post-conviction level. Such unrestrained punitive power is not only devastating to both the human condition and reentry, but it is wholly counterproductive to the advancement of public safety, which, afterall, is the purported mission of the DOC.

Supporting evidence for these claims will be derived from multiple sources. Class texts; <u>Crime and Punishment in American History</u>, <u>The Protestant Ethic and the Spirit of Punishment</u>, <u>Discipline and Punish,</u> and <u>HELLHOLE</u> will be used to correlate the concepts of isolation and punishment, while emphasizing Foucault's Panopticon as it applies to the inhibition of social contacts in the prison milieu. Specifically, how mail is opened, phone calls are recorded, and visits are physically and electronically surveilled. Scientific studies regarding prison visitation and solitary confinement will be reviewed, and DOC documents/ policies which prove to be hostile towards the formation and maintenance of prosocial relationships will also be cited. All of these resources will combine to answer the one overarching question of this paper: How do correctional policies in Massachusetts utilize multilayered forms of isolation, as extra-judicial punishment, to gradually bring about the social death of those within its custody?

Origins of Correctional Isolation

The origins of Massachusetts' isolation-based correctional policies can be traced back to the late eighteenth and early nineteenth centuries. During this period, a pivotal paradigm shift regarding punishment was taking place, as public shaming spectacles were largely abandoned in favor of more private and exclusive methods. Stanford law professor Lawrence M. Friedman describes how;

> New ideas about the sources of crime fed the urge to reform. They located the sources of deviant behavior in society itself, in the environment. But if society itself was corrupting, for some people, what was to be done? One solution was a kind of radical surgery; remove the deviant from his (weak and defective) family, his evil community, and put him in an artificially created and therefore corruption-free environment. From these notions sprang the penitentiary system. [3]

Consequently, the malevolent machinery of corrective social surgery had been irrevocably set in motion. To divide and conquer, through social isolation, became the law of the land.

Correctional apparatuses evolved rapidly and were all centered around punitive programs of isolation. Massachusetts opened its first prison, at Charlestown, in 1805, [4] and by 1878 it led the nation in the innovation of the probation system. [5] Friedman states that, during this structural build-up, "All the new penitentiaries, whatever their differences, were committed to silence, to a certain amount of isolation; and, more fundamentally, to discipline and regimentation. When the prisoner entered the gate, the staff stripped him of his individuality and reduced him to a common fate".[6]

Today, Massachusetts operates eighteen prison facilities, and the DOC has honed its horrible craft into an art form. Correctional authorities now employ four primary forms of isolation to induce the complete social death of those within its care: physical, emotional, psychological, and internalized. Each of these deadly components, then, merit careful review.

Physical Isolation & Social Death

Physical isolation is the first phase of social death, and it usually begins with one's arrest and confinement. Symbolically, the arrest process represents a total loss of power as well as autonomy. On a corporal plane, however, an arrest can be a painful affair, as law enforcement officers often utilize overly-aggressive tactics by which to subdue their suspects, even the non-violent ones. Theological scholar Mark Lewis Taylor notes that "The logic of enforcement is clear, knowing the seriousness of police plans is rooted in a spectacular seeing." [7] Therefore, arrests are dramatic by design so as to tangibly display state power as a dominant force. Regardless of the circumstances, an arrest is about subjugation, and it serves to physically remove a person from his or her own community while abruptly transplanting them to more alien environs. At this juncture, penal enslavement commences in concert with confinement.

Prison walls bluntly sever social ties by restricting access to social networks, but even more insidiously, by literally blotting-out all vestiges of surrounding society. Not only is a person unable to participate in civic life any longer, but he is also now cruelly blinded to its very existence and vice versa. It is the visual death of all that one once knew. Orlando Patterson posits "If the slave no longer belonged to a community, if he had no social existence outside of his master, then what was he? The initial response in almost all slave-holding societies was to define the slave as a socially dead person".[8] Certainly, some people may disagree with the equation of prisoners to slaves, but the parallels are undeniable. In fact, the thirteenth amendment to the United States Constitution actually codifies criminal slavery in declaring "Neither Slavery, nor involuntary servitude, except as a punishment for crime whereof the party shall have been duly convicted, shall exist within the United States, or any place subject to their jurisdiction".[9]

Armed with Constitutional authority, Massachusetts can justify the on-going dissection and physical degradation of its, largely minority, prison slave class. Initiation into its correctional institutions involves a systematic reduction of one's personhood, which includes, but is not limited to: uniform dress, numbered identification, solitary confinement, forceful restraint, strip searches, urine screens, constant supervision, and the censorship of communications. Patterson echoes the purpose of these policies in saying;

> The slave is violently uprooted from his milieu [arrested]. He is desocialized and depersonalized. This process of social negation constitutes the first, essentially external, phase of enslavement. The next phase involves the introduction of the slave into the community of his master [DOC], but it involves the paradox of introducing him as a non being [a number]. This explains the importance of law, custom, and ideology in the representation of the slave relation. [10]

Practices like these accomplish one thing; the extinction of social identity.

Social identity wanes within repressive systems of wanton disuse like prisons. Simon Clarke defines it as, "Social identity is about the category and attributes that a person is deemed to possess in relation to others".[11] Unfortunately, the austere physical isolation which correctional facilities impose upon those behind its walls does not allow for qualitative external relations to be fostered or reciprocated. Pre-existing relationships basically wither and die, crushed by the combined weight of physical distance, lengthy sentences, and hampered communicative abilities (especially in an ever-expanding digital world). Under such limited conditions, it becomes impossible to keep up with one's former life, so one is inevitably replaced in social circles and must suffer in silence as what should have been their starring role in life is now assumed by some other actor. Consequently, the course for even deeper isolation has been plotted.

Emotional Isolation

Emotional isolation is often characterized by a depressive out of sight - out of mind sensation, and is accompanied by feelings of hopelessness, frustration, and despair. As external relationships fall off like scabs, one must painfully turn their gaze from the ghosts of old allies to the social detritus which constitutes their new peer community. Correctional psychologist Craig Haney elucidates how;

> Prisoners who labor at both an emotional and behavioral level to develop a prison mask that is unrevealing and impenetrable risk alienation from themselves and others, may develop emotional flatness that becomes chronic and debilitating in social interaction and relationships, and find that they have created a permanent and unbridgeable distance between themselves and other people. [12]

Acclimatizing to a strange new social group, not of one's own choosing and in a harsh arena, while simultaneously anesthetizing oneself to external relational losses is not an easy task. However, assimilation is a feat which the DOC expects to be performed emotionlessly.

The emotional toll of isolation slowly murders the soul, as inter-personal losses mount. Every obliterated marriage, friendship, and family connection creates wounds which cannot be cauterized. Newly returned citizen Five Oman Mualimm-ak shares how "The scars that isolated confinement leaves behind may be invisible, but they are no less painful or permanent than physical scars".[13] No amount of internal camaraderie can ever adequately suture the trauma associated with social liquidation, and some have more to lose than others. Correctional researchers Grant Duwe and Valerie Clark point out how "For those who are married, visits with either spouses or children may be difficult because they create more stress and are often reminders of how their incarceration is preventing them from raising their children or providing for their families".[14] The emotional destabilization of entire families often leads to psychological detachment.

Psychological Isolation

Psychological isolation is most frequently correlated with solitary confinement, which can be a bit of a misnomer in that all forms of confinement are essentially solitary. French philosopher Michel Foucault encapsulates it as; "The crowd, a compact mass, a locus of multiple exchanges, individualities merging together, a collective effect, is abolished and replaced by a collection of separated individualities".[15] Every man is an island, so at this stage of isolation solitude becomes a matter of subjective gradation. Of course, solitary confinement is, as an institution, by far the most notorious and extreme form of correctional deprivation known to man. Afterall, there is something very chilling about the concept of a prison within a prison and the accelerated rate of self decay which it produces.

All DOC facilities possess some degree of solitary confinement, but two entire prisons, MCI Cedar Junction and Souza Baranowski CC, are devoted to housing a combined 1,948 maximum-security prisoners.[16] Solitary confinement is unnatural, to say the least, therefore it inspires equally abnormal adaptations by its subjects. However, the psychological cost of survival is incalculable. Atul Gawande highlights how "Without sustained social interaction, the human brain may become as impaired as one that has incurred a traumatic injury", [17] and he adds that "...simply to exist as a normal human being requires interaction with other people".[18] Perhaps the cruelest aspect of psychological isolation is how it erects new walls in the mind, breaching one's last line of defense. Clarke notes how "The actual walls of houses of confinement, of the madhouse and the asylum, created walls inside people as they feared the gap between the norms of rationality and their own potential madness."[19]

Internalized Isolation

Willfully placing human beings in solitary confinement is no different than throwing non-swimmers into the sea without life jackets, because both outcomes will be fatal. Radical segregation from even meager internal support systems, after the previously endured massacring of external relationships, is just too much for the psyche to bear. Gawande adds that "One of the paradoxes of solitary confinement is that, as starved as people become for companionship, the experience typically leaves them unfit for social interaction".[20] Mental unraveling marks the genesis of island fever, and without any other social sustenance to be found, the mind resorts to cannibalism in order to maintain a modicum of buoyancy. A general numbness sets in at this point, but the placid surface belies the maelstrom which is brewing inside.

The final form of correctional isolation is also the most distressing as it is of the internalized variety. Self-isolation is a defense mechanism which reduces an individual to the status of an automaton and results in complete social withdrawal. Haney insists;

A clear and consistent emphasis on maximizing visitation and supporting contact with the outside world must be implemented, both to minimize the division between the norms of prison and those of the free world, and to discourage dysfunctional social withdrawal that is difficult to reverse upon release.[21]

Considering that 92% of the prison population in Massachusetts will eventually be released, [22] it would appear advisable for the DOC to ensure that newly returning citizens be given more of a chance to swim than to sink once freed.

Reentry & Recidivism

Professor T. Richard Snyder boldly challenges the public consciousness regarding corporate responsibility for reentry by writing; "When we lose sight of the umbilical connection between criminal acts and the larger social collectivity, it is a simple step to deal with crime by dealing with the criminal as an isolate--a simple but tragic step. In so doing we make true redemption impossible, for redemption must include all within the scope of the symbiosis".[23] With this sentiment in mind, it becomes apparent that current DOC directives, which feature punitive forms of isolation, are diametrically opposed to meaningful reforms, hence the DOC's rather unspectacular 40% failure rate in terms of recidivism.[24] Imagine the depth of damage done to the socially dead who float around long enough to spy the shores of society, ever so briefly, only to be swept back out to an empty sea, again and again, by the cruel currents of recidivism.

As long as prisons are steered by cruel captains, the hulls of humanity will continue to be shattered upon the sharp shoals of punishment. Snyder relates how "A spirit of punishment permeates the prison; it cannot be escaped. There are oases, but for the majority prison is only a desert, a wilderness of punishment"[25]. Oddly enough, physical enslavement, emotional abandonment, psychological decay, and internalized withdrawal do not appear to lead towards the buried treasures of reentry and rehabilitation. How, then, is it possible for such counterintuitive correctional policies to continue unabated? The answer lies in the community's tacit approval of revenge-based punishment against those whom it defines as ontologically dead already. Snyder states, "The classifications of people of color as inferior and of criminals as garbage to be thrown away have combined to foster a response to crime that is one of vengeance and punishment".[26]

Policy Analysis

Ironically, the official DOC mission statement reads; "Promote public safety by managing offenders while providing care and appropriate programming in preparation for successful reentry into the community". [27.] However, like a misty mirage cresting upon a humid horizon, appearances can be deceiving. In reality, the DOC actually does more to undermine public safety than it does to promote it, and like all fear-based mechanisms of control the term itself is used as a blank check to euphemistically justify exclusionary punishments, such as; denial of visitation (conjugal and general), furloughs, and even family funeral attendance. Certainly, none of these sources of social contact can be honestly construed as risks to public safety. In fact, Duwe and Clark have proven the opposite to be true, reporting that" ... the public safety benefits resulting from increased social support for offenders - both in the institution and the community - would likely outweigh the costs involved to bring about systemic change" .[28]

A comparative analysis of DOC policies which inhibit and, in some instances, criminalize social contacts within correctional structures will reveal a startling disconnect between its stated mission and its actual practices. For example, the DOC mission claims to promote programming, but the Code of Massachusetts Regulations (CMR) severely prohibits any social contact between prisoners and volunteers. 103 CMR 430.24, Category 3-25 explicitly penalizes "Communicating directly or indirectly with any staff member or contract employee, volunteer, or a member of their family at their home address or telephone number, or for non-official business". Additionally, many volunteer programs (i.e. educational, self-help) are blanketed in anonymity clauses which impose a very impersonal power differential not conducive with trust-based relationship building.

If programming is "preparation for successful reentry into the community" as the DOC's mission statement claims, then why is the formation of positive, new relationships with volunteers, staff, mentors, and teachers (who are all members of the community themselves) so strictly contrabanded? Obviously, the DOC's position is to play their usual security trump card as a catch-all justification, but to what end does denying kind-hearted people (who may have worked with someone for years in various programs) the ability to even offer letters of support to the parole board? Any violations of what the DOC ambiguously defines as "Illegal Communication"[29] will result in the banishment of the volunteer and in disciplinary segregation time for the obviously incorrigible prisoner who presumed to make a friend by sending a message in a bottle while socially marooned.

Program invitations to external contacts are also inexplicably denied, which again illustrates the incongruity of DOC mission and policy. For instance, no known associates, friends, or family members are permitted entrance into DOC facilities beyond the visiting room. Therefore, the external social networks of prisoners are never afforded the opportunity to attend internal program functions which take place beyond standard boundaries. In an effort to bridge this social divide at MCI Norfolk, the Toastmasters program proposed to hold a special event in the visiting room so that friends and family members could share in the growth of their loved ones. The Director of Treatment replied "I am in receipt of your letter and special activity application dated February 19, 2012 requesting, for a second time, a Friends and Family Event for Toastmasters. Please be advised this request is denied. While I support the Toastmasters program, the ability to conduct a Friends and Family Event is not feasible at this time".[30]

Departmental regulations also target of inmate to inmate friendships. 103 CMR 481.21 (5) declares "The prohibition on inmate-to-inmate correspondence applies only to Department of Correction inmates incarcerated in a Department of Correction or county facility in Massachusetts". It stands to reason that once all external relationships have vanished, one would naturally seek friendship from those around him or her. Christine H. Lindquist affirms how "Social ties formed by inmates inside of their institution may develop into a crucial resource for dealing with the stressors associated with incarceration"[31]. In theory, internal social ties sound like they may be helpful, but prison populations are transient. Therefore, the diversity of sentences and the inability to control transfers basically stamps even these communions of the dead with an unknown expiration date.

Correctional policies extend beyond the walls, and any violations of them will result in a swift return to captivity. In an act of pure sadism, the

Massachusetts Parole Department requires that parolees not have any contact whatsoever with any other individuals who possess a criminal record.[32] Understandably, there is some legitimate concern over the maintenance of negative affiliations such as gangs, organized crime, or criminal conspiracies. However, to be forced to turn one's back on genuine friendships forged over years of shared struggles is just plain wrong. How can a person who knows all too well the pain of social abandonment be expected to visit such heartlessness upon a fellow castaway? Is criminality still thought to be contagious? Foucault responds that "Underlying disciplinary projects, the image of the plague stands for all forms of confusion and disorder; just as the image of the leper, cut off from all human contact, underlies projects of exclusion."[33]

Panoptic Communication

The DOC conditions compliance to its communication codes through the expert use of surveillance filters. Foucault describes his concept of the Panopticon, a powerful sense of scrutiny, as follows;

> Hence the major effect of the Panopticon: to induce in the inmate a state of conscious and permanent visibility that assures the automatic functioning of power. So to arrange things that the surveillance is permanent in its effects, even if it is discontinuous in its action ... in short, that the inmates should be caught up in a power situation of which they are themselves the bearers.[34]

The creation of inverted observation by correctional overseers represents a cunning ploy by which to make prisoners self-regulate their communications in mail, telephone calls, and visitation.

Corresponding with loved ones through traditional snail-mail in a digital e-mail age is like sending people antiques and vainly expecting reciprocity.

The fact is that free society simply does not utilize the United States Postal Service as its primary mode of communication anymore, and over 45% of what little mail which does still trickle into DOC facilities is just for personal money orders.[35] Therefore, receiving a piece of personal mail in 2014, despite the technological gap, can feel like a real lifeline from the free world. Of course, all incoming and out-going correspondence is subject to being: opened, searched, returned, fluroscoped (scanning device), read, and rejected as contraband depending on its contents. Such determinations are made by correctional staff who are authorized to do so under 103 CMR 481 mail regulations. Not knowing who else may be reading one's words or screening pictures of loved ones often induces self-editing to occur in true panoptic fashion.

Verbal communications are also problematic. While telephone calls may seem more convenient than snail-mail contacts, obstacles such as physical access and financial expense quickly dull the luster of this option. In DOC facilities, physical access to phones is restricted to certain times of the day, calls themselves are limited to twenty minutes, and prison overcrowding only further exacerbates the long lines of the socially marooned waiting to use them. In terms of expense, price-gouging by DOC service provider Global Tel Link (GTL) became so ridiculous, especially for long-distance calls, that the Federal Communications Commissions had to intervene.[36] On top of all this, the DOC employs auditory surveillance to listen to and record every call, which again causes individuals to be unnaturally scripted with their speech. The automatic functioning of power continues.

Prison visitation usually entails a small degree of physical contact, although some facilities only permit glass-partitioned visits, and as the only form of socialization which allows such closeness it is also the most heavily surveilled. Before even entering the visiting room, prisoners and their outside guests alike are searched and screened. Entrance procedures can be very subjectively applied, and 103 CMR 483.16 (1) states that "Any visitor, even one who has obtained prior permission to visit, may be denied entrance to the institution or told to terminate a visit and leave the premises. M.G.L. c.266.123 makes it a criminal trespass to refuse to leave an institution after being ordered by an officer to do so". Essentially, this ambiguous policy provides staff with broad powers of exclusion and discipline. Hypothetically, a person could be denied entrance for something as trivial as a wardrobe issue, and if they stick around to dispute their denial of access, they could then be criminally charged as punishment because the DOC does not negotiate with visitors.

DOC Commissioner, Luis S. Spencer, has recently added another layer of panoptic security to visitation procedures in the form of drug detecting canines. On the surface, such a policy seems to be reasonable as a means of deterring the introduction of drugs into the prison system. Spencer states that "While we realize that visits are an extremely important part of your lives during your incarceration, the Department will not allow your reentry and treatment efforts to be derailed by illicit activities"[37]. The insincerity of this statement is couched in the timing of its release, which was actually the DOC's response to the arrest of correctional staff for selling drugs to prisoners in MCI Norfolk's (CRA) drug recovery program. Ironically, Spencer's new drug detection policy does not apply to correctional staff members entering DOC facilities, but rather only punishes the friends and families who still dare to build bridges between the two worlds.

The cumulative impact of opened mail, recorded calls, and video-surveilled/dog-sniffed visits is the systematic discouragement of social contact. The Panopticon reigns supreme in diminishing the purity of human communication and interpersonal conduct with social networks. The daunting nature of maintaining prosocial relationships under such isolated conditions explains Professor Joshua C. Cochran's findings that "The most common visitation pattern prisoners experience is no visitation".[38] Afterall, who can honestly be expected to indefinitely endure the logistical challenges of time and distance, let alone the indignities of drug dogs, invasive searches, and stigmatization associated with supporting someone in prison. Ultimately, almost all contact wilts to a point of identity deficit beneath the punitive gaze of the DOC.

Extra-Judicial Punishment

Forensic psychiatrist Stuart Grassian, who has conducted studies in the Massachusetts DOC, calls it like it is in saying "Punish him, punish him, punish him: That's the only thing the correctional system knows to do".[39] Interestingly enough, the DOC does not operate under the auspices of the judiciary (as many people seem to believe), but is in fact an executive branch agency. [40] Therefore, the DOCs penchant for punishment is extra-judicial in nature as such penalties are inflicted at the post-conviction level, arbitrarily, by correctional authorities and not the courts. It is an important delineation to make, in that it raises some genuine ethical concerns regarding the abuses of state power. Namely, how can an institution like the DOC justify its use of extra-judicial tortures, like social isolation and solitary confinement, as being in alignment with its mandate of rehabilitation?

As far as the courts are concerned, public safety is satisfied during the criminal sentencing phase in which a person's period of social marooning is specified. Being sent to an artificial environment is itself considered to be the punishment. Everything that the DOC decides to apply after the fact is the equivalent of kicking someone while they are already down. Mualimm-ak articulates this well, stating.

> Everyone knows that prison is supposed to take away your freedom. But solitary doesn't just confine your body; it kills your soul. Yet neither a judge nor a jury of my peers handed down this sentence to me. Each of the tormented 23 hours per day that I spent in a bathroom-sized room, without any contact with the outside world, was determined by prison staff. [41]

The public requires justice, but the state demands the blood of social death.

Collateral Consequences

The DOC's use of extra-judicial assassination tactics against those within its care may be condoned by an apathetic public, but the sad reality is that these practices punish innocent bystanders as well. In the correctional war on crime the friends and families of the incarcerated become collateral consequences, thereby adding to the relational carnage which prison isolation creates. For every single social death that takes place within prisons, a ripple-effect occurs and multiplies the number of casualties beyond the walls exponentially. Braman avers, "Perhaps the most significant consequence of stigma among families of prisoners, then, is the distortion, diminution, and even severance of these social ties".[42] Lindquist adds how "... increasing proportions of jail and prison inmates translate into more spouses or children left behind on the outside, a population for whom the effects of incarceration are unknown". [43]

Surely, advocates of the current correctional system in Massachusetts will point out that prisons were not designed to be comfortable or accommodating atmospheres, and they would be right. People who have committed a crime must pay their debt to society, as this is what balances the scales of justice in America. Just how much human interest much be attached to this debt though? Must entire social networks be sacrificed to appease the insatiable appetites of correctional island gods? According to Braman's vision, " ... the difficult task that lies ahead is bringing offenders further into the social fold of family and community rather than removing them even further from it".[44] Restoring social bridges is the only way to reverse the Island Effect and its devastating consequences, because the human costs of continued isolation are too apocalyptic to consider.

Conclusion

The systematic social attrition occurring in modern correctional structures is appalling. In fact, state-sanctioned social cleansing policies which utilize; physical, emotional, psychological, and internalized forms of punitive isolation to eradicate the identities of those within its care are barbaric. By Grassian's accounting;

> In 2005, there were an estimated 81,600 prisoners in solitary in the U.S. That's 3.6 percent of the 2.2 million presently incarcerated ... Prison authorities in every state are running a massive uncontrolled experiment on them. And every day, the products of these trials trickle out on to the streets, with their prospects of rehabilitation professionally, socially, even physiologically diminished.[45]

Prisons have become human petri dishes, and the continued social decimation of prisoners and their corresponding support systems amounts to relational genocide.

Prison walls do much more than simply serve as ocean-like barriers which enforce the social marooning of those inside of them; they also provide the public with plausible deniability regarding the social holocaust simultaneously being carried out in the name of their safety. Atrocity is often fueled by secrecy, which may explain why prison walls are not constructed with transparent materials and why tourism is discouraged. Foucault illumines that "The Panopticon is a machine for dissociating the see/being seen dyad...",[46] so the fact that no one is watching the watchers grants them the license to kill at will. Therefore, the ontological culling of the "criminal" class proceeds, unchecked, via the isolation and social starvation of community castaways. If "correction" is accomplished through the existential evisceration and extinction of individual identities and social networks, then the Massachusetts DOC is an exemplary institution.

Endnotes

1. MA DOC <u>Strategic Plan 2010-2015</u>. Print.
2. Braman, Donald. <u>Invisible Punishment: The Collateral Consequences of Mass Imprisonment</u>. New Press.2002.New York,NY.(PP.135).Print.
3. Friedman, Lawrence M. <u>Crime and Punishment in American History</u>. Basic Books.1993.New York,NY.(PP.77)Print.
4. ibid (79)
5. ibid (163)
6. ibid (79)
7. Taylor, Mark Lewis. <u>The Executed God</u>. Minneapolis, MN.(PP.34).Print.
8. Patterson, Orlando. <u>Slavery and Social Death</u>. Harvard University Press. (PP.38).Print.
9. United States Constitution. Amendment 13, Section 1. Ratified December 6, 1865.Print.
10. Patterson, Orlando. (38)
11. Clarke, Simon. <u>Culture and Identity</u>. Sage Handbook of Cultural Analys.2008.(PP.512). Print.
12. Haney, Craig.
13. Mualimm-ak,Five Oman. <u>Solitary Confinement's Invisible Scars</u>. Prison Legal News.February 2 14.(PP.48).Print.
14. Duwe, Grant. Clark, Valerie. <u>Blessed Be the Social Tie That Binds:The Effects of Prison Visitation on Offender Recidivism</u>. Sage.Criminal Justice Policy Review.2013. (PP.290) .Print.
15. Foucault, Michel. <u>Discipline and Punish</u>. 2nd Ed. Vintage.1995.New York,NY.(PP.201).Print.
16. MA DOC <u>Strategic Plan 2010-2015</u>. Print.
17. Gawande, Atul. <u>HELLHOLE</u>. The New Yorker.March 30, 2009.(PP.4).Print.
18. ibid (1)
19. Clarke, Simon. (515)
20. Gawande, Atul. (7)
21. Haney,Craig. (88)
22. MA DOC <u>Strategic Plan</u> 2010-2015. Print.
23. Snyder, T. Richard. <u>The Protestant Ethic and the Spirit of Punishment</u>.Wm.B.Eerdmans.2001.Grand Rapids,MI.(PP.71).Print.
24. MA DOC <u>Strategic Plan</u> 2010-2015. Print.
25. Snyder,T.Richard. (5)
26. ibid (54)
27. MA DOC <u>Strategic Plan</u> 2010-2015.Print.
28. Duwe,Grant. (292) Clark,Valerie.

29. 103 CMR 430.24 & 103 CMR 481
30. Sweeney,Kelley. Internal Letter from MCI Norfolk D.O.T. March 28, 2012.Print.
31. Lindquist,Christine H. Social Integration and Mental Well-Being Among Jail Inmates, Springer. Sociological Forum,Vol.15,No.3. September 2000.(PP.436).Print.
32. 120 CMR 300.07 (2) Parole
33. Foucault,Michel. (199)
34. ibid (201) *Panopticon adapted from Jeremy Bentham's original.
35. Keefe Commissary Network RFR Contract Bid. (PP .113). Print.
36. Prison Legal News.February 2014.Print.
37. Spencer,Luis S. DOC Memo Support. March 6, 2013. Print.
38. Cochran, Joshua C. Breaches in the Wall: Imprisonment, Social Support, and Recidivism. Journal of Research in Crime and Delinquency.2014.(PP.205).Print.
39. Grassian,Stuart. Going Crazy in Solitary. THE WEEK.March 28,2014.(PP.41).Print.
40. MA DOC Strategic Plan 2010-2015.Print.
41. Mualimm-ak,Five Oman. (118)
42. Braman,Donald. (131)
43. Linquist,Christine fL (433)
44. Braman,Oonald (135)
45. Grassian,Stuart (40)
46. Foucault,Michel. (201-202)

Capitalism and Ontological Otherness in Modern-Day America

Shaun

How does capitalism, as a bedrock of American society and economy today, reinforce and perpetuate historical racist and Calvinist-influenced notions of the criminal 'other', while legitimizing and engendering a new form of ontological othering within the context of mass incarceration?

Abstract

From a social perspective, the notion of the criminal ontological other is one of the foremost roots of mass incarceration in America -- it has taken hold of public consciousness (and indeed, public sub consciousness) to the point where society routinely and gladly hands over millions of its people to be locked up for large periods of time. The notion of the ontological 'criminal' is rooted in historical racism and notions of Calvinist falseness, both of which have come to set the foundation for this phenomenon in the present day, through implicit bias. However, the developing sense of otherness towards the 'criminal' is redefined, perpetuated, and legitimized by a more present phenomenon in society nowadays: capitalism. By naturalizing 'productivity' as a metric for defining a person's worth, capitalism directly engenders and legitimizes a notion of the poor and unproductive as a 'criminal' other. By providing a market for both indirect and direct stakeholders to profit and benefit from the notion of the 'criminal', capitalism also incentivizes and perpetuates the continuation of this construct. The overwhelming result is that society has subconsciously defined a group of 'ontological others' within itself, which it then willingly incarcerates en masse.

Introduction - Mass Incarceration in America Today

The United States of America today is in a crisis of punishment. Over two million people are in prison today; factoring in people who are under parole and probation, the number reaches a staggering 7.1 million (Prins, 2007). In 2007, $74 billion was spent on corrections (Kyckelhahn, 2010), with more full-time employees working in American corrections than in any Fortune 500 company save General Motors (Parenti, 213). And yet, while awareness of (and concern over) the *costs* of the incarceration machine in America has been on a rise, this trend is by no means on a downturn. Many societal and economic factors have been implicated in being responsible for the extent of mass incarceration today, including the prison-industrial complex that has developed -- the complex of financial and economic interests (of law enforcement officers, prison construction firms, private prison corporations, and numerous other stakeholders and investors) whose well being is dependent on the size of the prison population (Dyer, 3). It is easy to cast responsibility for this crisis on the impersonal and amoral workings of profit-driven industries, but there is more to this phenomenon than simply raw desire to profit on the parts of these stakeholders. Although the new prisons being built have been wildly profitable for the prison-industrial complex, it is not only the supply of prisons that is driving this hunger to incarcerate; remarkably, demand for new prisons has been so high that these new facilities have been filled as soon as they have been built, with most prison jurisdictions filled over capacity (Dyer, 5). Society -- consisting of the voters who empower politicians in defining sentencing policies -- is equally (and perhaps more) culpable in its willingness to hand over large portions of its population to be locked up and put away for long periods of time. This fear of 'criminals', and eagerness to separate ourselves from law-breakers, may be ascribed to a few factors -- preeminently among which is the notion of the ontological other.

In this paper, I will examine the roots of the ontological other in American society today, focusing specifically and predominantly on capitalism as a force that creates and legitimizes a new form of othering, while empowering historical notions of the 'other' in a way that perpetuates the other-ness of the 'criminal'. However, in elucidating this relationship, a few key terms will first have to be defined. Capitalism refers to the economic system centered around the notion of the market, comprising buyers and sellers competing over goods, as a model for society to function. This affects not just the economy but also society at large, as people come to be viewed within their roles as factors of production, consumers, or producers. The term 'criminal' refers to a person who has been found guilty of breaking a law, leading to his or her incarceration. This is contrasted with the notion of the 'good person', the archetypal (productive) middle-class American who has not been arrested or incarcerated over a transgression of the law. As I will show, however, the label 'criminal' has also come to be associated with being of lesser value and worth, being inherently *worse* than a 'good person'; I therefore also use these terms to describe the social dichotomy arising from ontological othering. Ontological othering occurs when a person (or group of people) fails to identify with a person or particular class of people, usually seeing oneself as being fundamentally (and ontologically) distinct, separate, and often superior to the members of the outgroup. This defined itself in American history within the context of racism, and salvation and fallenness in Calvinist Protestant ideology (Snyder, 13-14), but, especially as directed towards the criminal, has come to take on a new areligious and legitimate bent in America. Finally, the technical sociological term 'outgroup' refers to a group of people who constitute the 'other' in society, used in contrast to the 'ingroup', the majority in society who performs the othering.

A few primary motivations guide and invest my interest in capitalism as a root of the criminal ontological other. Primarily, if we seek to repair the criminal justice system by educating society and deconstructing the notion of the other, we first have to understand what it is really driven by in society. Racist and Calvinist notions, as have been extensively implicated in this phenomenon, may contribute towards implicit bias and support for this notion, but they seem to present an incomplete picture. I realize this also because, as a Singaporean, I spent the vast majority of my years in a culture which has neither historical associations with slavery and institutional racism nor any significant Christian (let alone Calvinist) influence. Indeed, if anything, as a country of recent immigrants from various parts of East and South Asia (most Singaporean citizens are no more than third- or fourth-generation citizens), the social structure of Singaporean society is more significantly influenced by Confucius than Calvin. Yet, this notion of the criminal other as an ontologically inferior caste still exists powerfully. As an officer in the Singapore Police Force, who will face and interact with "criminals" for most of my life, I am also deeply interested and invested in discovering why the notion of the criminal other is so endemic, even across societies. Finally, deeply personally, some of the people in my life for whom I have come to attain deepest respect are the incarcerated people I have class with every week, in Norfolk MCI. These men are not the criminals that I have been conditioned to believe belong in a prison. I am eager to discover why society believes that people are ontologically corrupt and inferior simply because they were convicted of breaking a law.

Methodology

To explore the causal relationship between the criminal ontological other and the large scale embracing of capitalism that has come to be a way of life by American society, I will begin with a general understanding of the ontological other in mass incarceration, and work towards a specific analysis of capitalism in this situation. First, I will set the framework for the discussion by examining the relationship between ontological otherness and mass incarceration, showing how mass incarceration is supported by the notion of the other, despite it being illusory and misguided. In this context, then, I will then briefly discuss how two historical factors have set the context and foundation for the ontological other in society today -- specifically, how the racism and racial bias that has gripped America for centuries, and the Protestant Calvinist notions of fallenness, original sin, and redemption by grace have given rise to the caste of ontologically corrupt 'criminals'. However, while acknowledging the significance of these factors in generating implicit bias, I will show how the embracing of capitalism has radically changed and redefined this phenomenon by empowering, legitimizing, and perpetuating this preexisting notion of the other in two subtle, but more extensive ways. Specifically, I will examine how capitalism both directly builds the notion of the 'other' in society, and how it motivates the continued existence of this outgroup through the market. I will then conclude with the implications of this phenomenon for society nowadays.

Ontological Otherness and Mass Incarceration in Modern-Day America

As introduced earlier, the monetary and economic benefit of running prisons is certainly beneficial to stakeholders of the prison-industrial complex, but it cannot function without the complicity of society in being eager to lock up the people it deems inferior. Not surprisingly, this eagerness finds its root in the notion of the criminal ontological other. It is the means by which society justifies separating certain groups of people from the larger society -- if 'criminals' are actually different and inferior as compared to the 'good people' in society, it is much more conscionable to grant them different and inferior treatment. Presupposing that there is something intrinsically criminal (and corrupt) about the person who breaks the law, ontological otherness means that if someone transgresses in this manner, the person is not a worthy 'good person', and is part of the 'other'. In this way, the 'criminal' person comes to be defined entirely and ontologically not by his or her worth in person-hood but by his or her transgression, as a societal 'wretch' (Snyder, 53). And because society has (for various reasons) come to fear these wretches as part of a vile and dangerous outgroup, it is eager to cast lawbreakers into vile and dangerous conditions in the prison system, because that is what befits them (Yousman, 127). When the 'good people' in society stop identifying themselves in common personhood with the people who are convicted of breaking the law, society becomes unable to empathize with its 'criminals'. With this lack of empathy, it is then just one small further step to punish and lock these 'criminals' up en masse.

However, this notion of the criminal other is illusory and misguided -- in the way that mass incarceration operates in America (and perhaps in general), it is not only wretches that inhabit prisons. Foucalt, in *Discipline and Punish,* explains this through the illustration of a what he calls a 'carceral network' (301) that all in society live in -- we like to think that incarceration is only for the unassimilable in society, but ultimately, all members of society are under the same network and system of control and punishment, that ranges from disapproval over breaking social etiquette to incarceration over breaking laws. A 'criminal' breaking a law, as Foucalt explains, is simply further down the spectrum from a 'good person' making a transgression of etiquette; depending on the severity of the transgression, 'good people' can find themselves very easily "[passing] naturally from disorder to offense and back [and] from a transgression of the law to a slight departure from a rule, an average, a demand, a norm" (Foucalt, 298). Indeed, contrary to the idea that it is only 'criminals' who behave in criminal ways, Mark Taylor astutely notes in *The Executed God: The Way of the Cross in Lockdown America* that "it is not unusual for those who are in the *outer prison* to find that certain life crises, certain traumas, can easily and expectedly catapult ['good people'] into the real prison of razor wire, Plexiglas, steel and guards... Although many previously had thought themselves to be quite other to the world of the imprisoned, they learn that the journey is not quite so discontinuous as they thought from the world of one regimen to another" (Taylor, 44).

As pertains to the American incarceration system, both Taylor and Foucalt are overwhelmingly accurate. The notion that prisons contain a class of people who are more violent, more corrupt, and more evil -- in other words, ontologically inferior -- is far less reflective of the actual situation than people would like to think. For example, it is convenient to look to high recidivism rates as evidence that a 'criminal' is, and always will be a criminal, but the reality is that the vast majority of recidivists are rearrested for nonviolent offenses in America, and a similar majority of parolees or probationers who are re-arrested are arrested because of a small violation of one of many restrictions and rules that govern their closely-monitored lives as exiles (such as paying fines or meeting with probation officers) (Alexander, 94-95). A majority of the people in prison are also incarcerated for non-violent offenses. The ontological profiles of a vast majority of the 'criminals' are not very different from that of the rest of society. The social construct of the identity of the criminal other, however, has become very defined and distinct -- one that has its foundation in centuries of othering throughout American history.[1] I refer here to the ontological profile, in terms of corruption and inferiority in being, not other profiles (socioeconomic, ethnic, etc.) in which the profiles of the 'criminals' do differ from the rest of society, as will be discussed further on.

Racism and Calvinism as Historical Foundations for the Modern Ontological Other

Although the notion of the ontological other has only manifested itself with new (and legitimized) ferocity towards the 'criminal' in recent history, it has existed in America for centuries, arising from two major sources: racism and Calvinist Protestant ideology.

Since colonial times, racism has been endemic in American society -- from the institution of chattel slavery, where Africans were shipped en masse to America to serve as slaves for whites (as was deemed fitting with their purported phrenological inferiority), to the post-Abolition Reconstruction period, to the institution of the Jim Crow laws which officiated the second-class status of African Americans, American society has suffered under the pall of seemingly persistent racist othering. Beginning in white supremacy, racism has always been a force behind the othering of people of color. Today, racism has become less overt in America, probably due to education, and the fact that it has become politically incorrect to be a white supremacist. However, as Michelle Alexander argues in *The New Jim Crow: Mass Incarceration in the Age of Colorblindness*, "Most people assume that racism, and racial systems generally, are fundamentally a function of attitudes... The widespread and mistaken belief that racial animus is necessary for the creation and maintenance of radicalized systems of social control is the most important reason that [America has] remained in deep denial" (Alexander, 183). Indeed, although racism and racial animus are far less overt and seemingly far less present in American society nowadays, the structures that oppressed African Americans for centuries linger in the subconscious of society to give rise to implicit bias and othering of minority races, especially towards African Americans. This is seen in many areas of society in which blacks -- especially young, black men -- have been socially and economically marginalized because they are subconsciously perceived as inferior or as threats (Forman, 111). However, it is most apparent in the criminal justice system, where a grossly disproportionate number of those incarcerated and punished are people of color (Alexander, 6). Indeed, because society is officially colorblind, it is "no longer permissible to hate blacks", but interestingly, "we are encouraged to [hate criminals]" (Alexander, 199). The ontological status of the inferior black person in history has set a firm precedent for the inferior caste of 'criminals' today.

A second source of othering that has existed and developed through America's history is that arising from the Calvinist Protestant notion of redemption and fallenness. Calvinism, the branch of Protestantism that emphasizes the depravity of all humankind through original sin, and the salvation of some of them -- the elect -- through the free and unmerited grace of God, was a central school of belief in colonial Protestant America. With many in the early American colonies holding to these ideas, the classifications of "fallen" and "redeemed" began to be applied in reference to essential (and ontological) being rather than simply in reference to behavior, dividing the members of society into saved and condemned people -- good and depraved, persons and non persons (Snyder, 47). The saved people, then, felt a sense of ontological superiority over the fallen 'sinners' who appeared to be unsaved, which fit well with the view that the white supremacists already had over their black slaves -- black slaves were viewed by the whites as unredeemed and lost, people who could be treated differently from the redeemed (Snyder, 49). Of course, America today is officially secular and Americans are certainly much less Calvinist (or even religious) than their ancestors. However, as Snyder remarks, one does not "have to be theologically aware or intentional to be influenced by the spirit of a theology that has become part of the secular air" that society breathes (Snyder, 30). Just as the ontological outgroup of the racially inferior person of color has found a new outlet in the ontological othering of the 'criminal', it is not difficult to see how ontology that dictates righteousness and corruptness could set the foundation for defining the ontology of the 'criminal'.

These two factors contextualize the history of ontological othering in America, showing how the association of the 'criminal' with corruption and ontological inferiority could take root so quickly, easily, and extensively. However, there is a gap between the ontological othering that is seen against the 'criminal' today, and the othering that is accounted for by these historical factors. Firstly, although the outgroup comprising the 'criminals' overlaps significantly with the outgroup comprising people of color, the ontological caste of the 'criminal' does not impact middle- and upper-class educated African Americans in the same way that it impacts lower-income African Americans (Forman, 132). As this is not accountable for by Calvinist notions of salvation (the dichotomy here exists in terms of wealth and social status, rather than religious affiliation or moral goodness), there seems to be an additional economic factor at work which exacerbates the way *poor* African Americans are othered by society. Furthermore, implicit bias -- the spirit of theology that has become part of the secular air that we breathe, and the spirit of racism that has come to subconsciously mar the racial equality and colorblindness that we profess -- may have set the historical foundation for the notions of the other and explain why it still lingers below the superficial public consciousness, but it will not advance and develop the sense of othering in itself, because the historical factors that drive them are themselves no longer being significantly furthered. Indeed, the fervor with which society is relegating some of its members into the ontological caste of the 'criminal' points towards a separate phenomenon that is at work in extending, redefining, and even legitimizing this notion of the ontological other in society nowadays: capitalism.

Capitalism Reinforces, Redefines, Secularizes, and Legitimizes Notions of the Other

As an economic system that has come to be thoroughly and wholeheartedly embraced by American society, capitalism strengthens preexisting notions of the ontological other while engendering a new and legitimized form of it in two major ways. First, as a social and societal structure, it directly engenders notions of the 'other' in itself, adding to preexisting notions while legitimizing them. Second, as an economic structure, it thrives on the continued existence of the outgroup (criminal or not), providing a force that motivates and perpetuates ontological othering in society. Capitalism directly engenders and strengthens notions of the other, as a social structure. Given the extent to which capitalist ways of thinking have shaped American public consciousness and have come to be accepted as right and natural, it is no surprise that it has also directly redefined the notion of the ontological other as a societal construct. Just as the target outgroup of Calvinism comprises sinners, and the target outgroup of racism comprises people of color, the target outgroup of capitalism consists of the poor and unproductive (unskilled) in society. Because capitalism prizes competition, effectiveness and productivity, people have inadvertently come to be viewed in terms of their effectiveness in the market -- as producers, consumers, or as factors of production. With the market in capitalism enshrined as the pinnacle of development, and the means by which maximum welfare and benefit (essentially, material *eudaimonia*) can be achieved, the worth of an individual to society has come to be very closely approximated by their productivity in their roles in it. For example, people who are released from incarceration are often given the charge to be '*productive* members of society'. When introducing oneself at social events, it is common to include a description of one's occupation or vocation in society. Part-time workers (people who are drawing income but are arguably less 'productive' members of society) have been found to be almost 50% more likely to suffer from depression than full-time workers, according to a 2013 study by Gallup (Ivans, 2013). Because the capitalism that has arrested public consciousness has also come to define worth in America, the poor and unskilled, being of less value to the capitalist economy, end up being of less value overall, forming a distinct ontological outgroup to society.

In addition, capitalism exacerbates this phenomenon and distinction because it physically separates and isolates people according to their wealth (corresponding to levels of productivity). Capitalism rewards the productive and richer members of society with material wealth and comfort, while the unproductive and poorer members of society are dealt a comparatively more meager standard of living. Since neighborhoods tend to be organized according to desirability for the social class of its inhabitants, and property in 'rich' estates come to be out of reach of poorer people, society is stratified with richer people living in separate neighborhoods, towns, and worlds from poorer people. As a result, the problem of richer people regarding the poor as unproductive and less worthy is aggravated, because interaction between the ingroup and the outgroup gets reduced. This perpetuates a vicious cycle in which the ingroup of society becomes increasingly isolated and decreasingly able to identify with the poor outgroup, increasing the sense of othering experienced because of a lack of familiarity and identification. As Ivan Goldman notes in *Sick Justice*, "most middle-class people don't know anyone in the penitentiary system and thus tend to think of inmates as the other, a dangerous, barely human type best kept behind bars" (20). On the other hand, people in poorer communities regularly see young (black) men being swept off the streets into prisons. Coupled with the demonization they and their peers face by the ingroup, these people, already in the outgroup, tend to the embrace their stigmatized identity as an "other" to the rest of society. This manifests itself in phenomena like pride in the "gangsta rap" culture and the acceptance of the fact that their lives are, and will be, closely interwoven with the prison system (Alexander, 174-175). Eventually, the overwhelming effect is a sense of distance, unfamiliarity, fear, and otherness between the poor outgroup and the middle- to upper-class ingroup.

As a result of capitalism as a way of thinking and assessing worth, and capitalism as a system which stratifies people according to their wealth and productivity, it seems almost inadvertent that a large scale embracing of capitalism by society would lead to the othering of poor and unproductive people. This then feeds directly and powerfully into the othering of the 'criminal'. Since poor and unproductive people are of less economic and ontological value, society is also more willing to separate these people from the majority (i.e. lock them up). This is made clear when studying the demographic trends of incarcerated people -- state prisoners average just a tenth-grade education, about 70% have no high school diploma, and incarceration rates fall about twenty-fold for college graduates as compared to high-school dropouts, even after controlling for other factors like age and ethnicity (Western & Pettit, 2010). Very clearly, there is a strong correlation between educational level (a marker of productivity to society) and purported criminality,[2] closely mirroring the conflation of the outgroups of the criminal and the unproductive. This is certainly not a coincidence. As Taylor observes, incarcerated people tend to come from disenfranchised and 'other' groups which society sees as surplus and expendable. These people in the 'other' class are then moved into prisons where they are trained more intensely to adopt that identity, and when they return to society and their (usually) poorer communities once again, their presence and concentration there becomes additional reasons to justify the further criminalization and othering of people in these entire neighborhoods, in general (Taylor, 49, 62). Criminal ontological othering is so closely and inextricably intertwined with the ontological othering of the poor that the two groups are essentially inseparable, as they perpetuate each other. Upon examination, this makes sense. Given that capitalism has come to be key in defining American society, it is natural that the outgroup from capitalism would assimilate the preexisting outgroups comprising people of color and people who are 'sinful', and then redefine the *general* outgroup for society's condemned -- the 'criminals'.

To be sure, there is not a complete overlap between the outgroup of the poor and the 'criminals' -- there certainly are 'criminals' from more 'productive' sectors of society, who are also othered along with the poorer and more 'unproductive' people found guilty of breaking the law. Here, we must recognize that the outgroup of the poor reinforces the outgroup of the 'criminals' because of the association between the two, but they are not identical. However, we must also remember that when a "productive" person breaks a law (for example, by stealing, or by raping, thereby hurting the overall productivity of the community), the person ceases to be productive, and is thence perceived as a threat to the overall productivity of the society. The notions of criminality and lack of productivity *are* very closely related. Regardless, in any form of othering by proxy (in this case, othering 'criminals' as a proxy for othering poor and unproductive people), there is inevitably an imperfect overlap. Curiously, however, because society has come to generally associate the two groups into the same outgroup, the areas of *non*-overlap are ignored, and the perceived traits of one outgroup become conflated with that of the other. All unproductive people hence become associated with criminality, and 'criminals' in general become associated with a lack of productivity.

This association, which ascribes 'criminals' the trait of a lack of productivity, is of tremendous significance; indeed, therein lies the the power and legitimacy -- the key -- of capitalism as a means for society to other the 'criminal' caste. Through capitalism, society does not (overtly) discriminate and ascribe worth to people according to arbitrary grace given by God, nor does it do so according to the race that a person is arbitrarily born into. Rather, society creates its outgroup and justifies it based on something that is apparently extremely non-arbitrary, justified, and fair: one's measurable contribution to the economic success of a secular (and capitalist) society. Indeed, the notion that one's status in society is a measure of one's work and effort is powerful -- it convinces the ingroup that the status of any individual in the outgroup is something the person has brought upon himself or herself (Goldman, 148-149), the just desserts as doled out by the fair and unbaised invisible hand.[3] Because the unproductive person is seen to have brought poverty upon himself or herself, capitalism legitimizes the sense of superiority towards and otherness on the poor classes; since poorness and the 'criminal' status are conflated, 'criminals' are seen to deserve their lower estate in society. In this way, it becomes conscionable to discriminate against and *other* the 'criminal' outgroup, while enjoying one's status as part of the 'good person' ingroup. Capitalism, as an economic structure, motivates the existence of the 'other'

Furthermore, capitalism does not only build upon preexisting notions to directly engender its own legitimized form of the 'criminal' ontological other. As an economic structure, its markets thrive on the existence of the outgroup in society; hence, it also motivates and insures the continued existence of the criminal 'other' by ensuring that society, through its primary and secondary stakeholders in crime control and law enforcement, is incentivized to sustain this bias against 'criminals'.

The secondary and indirect stakeholders in the market of crime prevention are the news and entertainment media industries that benefit from the existence of an unfamiliar, and hence fearsome, caste of 'criminals' around whom drama and sensation can be generated. In a study done by Bill Yousman examining all 4798 prison and penal system-related news stories reported on ABC, CBS, and NBC in the years 1990, 1995 and 2000, 52% of all the stories centered around just three primary themes: violent unrest and riots in prison, stories about prison escapes, and stories about the growing prison population -- the ever-growing class of 'criminals' (Yousman, 78). In all of these media reports, Yousman identified some messages that ran through all of them, including that 1) Prisoners are dangerous individuals who should be feared, 2) society therefore needs prisons to keep ordinary citizens safe, and that 3) prisoners deserve the punishment that is meted out to them (Yousman, 81). People are drawn to dramatic portrayals of the 'criminal' other and the exploits of this fearsome and unfamiliar group, and news outlets benefit monetarily from the attention received when they report such stories. In a 1997 study by the University of Miami's Communications School, it was found that crime coverage on the local news network took up double the airtime of reports on politics, education, and health combined (Dyer, 109). Because of the way in which the invisible hand in capitalism allocates resources -- according to demand and supply of goods – Joel Dyer notes in *The Perpetual Prisoner Machine* that there has been a "not so subtle shift from important information to profitable information in the 'what-is-news' equation" (Dyer, 73). Reporting sensational and other-inducing news on crime is profitable, making news broadcasting agencies indirectly dependent on the existence of the idea of the 'criminal' to generate profits.

This phenomenon, in which industries benefit from the existence of the 'criminal' outgroup, is not only isolated to news broadcasting outlets; it is also seen (much more apparently) in the movie and television producers of the entertainment industry. In the first *Die Hard* movie, there were only 18 deaths, in the second, there were 264. *Robocop* killed off 32 bad guys in the first time movie, but slaughtered 81 in his second. The films *The Godfather, The Godfather II,* and *Godfather III* killed 12, 18, and 53 respectively (Dyer, 76). This pattern arises because movie and TV producers are increasingly realizing that death, violence, and criminality as a whole are surefire ways to guarantee returns on their investment, since violence is arresting to the viewer and is therefore profitable (Dyer, 75). This demand for violence, crime, and action possesses a tremendous amount of force because producers realize the massive incentives and profits that the market provides to those who can meet this demand. Therefore, they are indirectly invested, as secondary stakeholders in the criminal justice network, in the continued existence of the 'criminal' other in society.

Furthermore, this motivating force for the perpetuation of the ontological other is especially potent, because the hunger in this market is self-reinforcing -- producers increase the frequency and drama of such presentations because it is profitable to do so, but in feeding (and increasing) the appetite of the public for such crime-related drama, they also reinforce and cement the idea of the criminal other. Consumers of crime-oriented movies and television shows, designed to increase ratings and profits, experience an exaggerated apprehension of crime and fear of 'criminals', in line with studies showing that the majority of Americans now base their worldview more on mediated messages shown on television than on their own firsthand observations (Dyer, 3). And indeed, these mediated messages (intentionally or not) are messages that feed the notion of the criminal as an 'other'. In many of the television programs about law enforcement and order, the protagonists are criminal justice workers and professionals -- lawyers, police officers, judges -- and the incarcerated people who do appear in the shows tend to be one-dimensional plot devices meant to advance the protagonists' stories, rather than real characters (Yousman, 114). The overwhelming result of this is that the 'criminal' is gradually seen less and less as a person, and more as an 'other' whom the public cannot identify with. In this way, in addition to incentivizing the continuation of the notion of the other by providing profits towards that end, the capitalist structure of the economy also incidentally and conveniently sustains these notions in the process, happily securing and insuring the perpetuation of the idea of the ontological other in society.

In addition, the market structure of capitalism, which operates solely on profit-driven responses to demand and supply, also causes immediate and *primary* stakeholders -- law enforcement agencies, and the investors in the prison-industrial complex -- to benefit from law-breakers being perceived as an ontological other. For indeed, the market for 'correcting' these 'criminals' is profitable – in 2007, $74 billion was spent on corrections (Kyckelhahn, 2010); in Colorado, because private prisons are paid $5 to $7 per hour per person by companies who make use of prison labor, and because they pay the workers as little as $0.23 to $1.15 per hour, the private prison pockets $3.62 million a year simply by overseeing the labor environment (Dyer, 233). Because the prison-industrial complex is so large and profitable, crime figures reported by the FBI and Justice Department are monitored by Wall Street analysts as closely as unemployment rates and quarterly earnings reports are monitored, because they have come to be the leading indicators for the forecast of numerous stocks and investment trusts that are devoted to prison projects (Dyer, 23). The amount of profit generated around incarcerating people is massive, and it is easy to see why it would be extremely profitable to keep 'criminals' being perceived to be dangerous and necessary to be locked up -- so that the demand for these institutions to lock them up is sustained, allowing the prison-industrial complex to continue to thrive. The economy is invested in keeping people afraid and distanced from the 'criminals', because jobs are secured and productivity is generated if there is a demand for protection and segregation of these people from the general society. Dyer observed that as a result of the portrayal of law-breakers as violent, fearsome, and unfamiliar in the dramatized news content that are designed specifically to lure viewers, there has been a much greater feeling of insecurity and dependence on law enforcement for safety (111). Jobs are created as a byproduct of othering the 'criminal', and prisons profit as a result of othering the 'criminal'. The direct stakeholders in the law enforcement industries live off society othering the 'criminal'; in this way, capitalism, as an economic structure, strongly motivates the the othering of the 'criminal'.

In these ways, the market mechanism of capitalism incentivizes the continued presence of ontological othering in society because of the benefit that it affords to many stakeholders in society -- both primary and secondary. Because of the legitimization of the sense of othering as discussed earlier, there is little disincentive to deconstruct such notions to begin with; with such economic motivations, any disincentives that *do* exist come to be weighed against the overwhelming incentives of keeping the notion of the 'criminal' other intact. As a result, the capitalist market economy strongly supports the idea of ontological criminality, and, because it is invested in its continuation, perpetuates and reinforces these ideas through society (deliberately or not).

Capitalism and Ontological Othering -- Summary

In summary, capitalism reinforces and strengthens the institution of the ontological other in two main ways. As a societal structure, it builds on preexisting notions from Calvinism and racism to directly engender its own legitimized outgroup, comprising poor and unproductive people as the "criminal" ontological other. As an economic structure that thrives on the continued existence of this class of the "other", it also motivates and incentivizes the continued definition of the ontological 'criminal'. In conjunction, it presents a formidable force that not only allows society to legitimately (and in good conscience) view a particular subgroup of people as the 'other', but also fits into and draws momentum from preexisting inclinations and biases that are dormant in society -- the poor person, the black person, and the sinner can all fit into the mold of the 'criminal' as the single societal outgroup. And because of the profitable stake that capitalist America has in sustaining and perpetuating the notion of the 'other', capitalism provides an added layer of guarantee and incentive that ensures the existence of the outgroup, should ontological prejudices and biases wane. The result is that American society today willingly hands over millions of people to be put away and put out of sight for long periods of time, because it systematically and endemically treats a particular class of people -- the 'criminals' -- as different, as the 'other'. And perhaps most troublingly, because of the way in which this system is so entrenched and legitimized by capitalism, society does not realize it. Perhaps some do, but they do not see anything wrong with it. And even they did, there is no significant desire to change it.

Conclusions and Implications

The first step to solving a problem is to first understand the problem; the first step in addressing an enemy is to first discover who the enemy is. In this paper, I have sought to uncover the 'enemy' by exploring the reasons why society has reached a point where it systematically views one group of people as different, as dangerous, as inherently more corrupt, and inherently more deserving of being locked up than others. Based on preexisting and implicit biases borne from religious ideology and racist tension, capitalism has taken the notion of the ontological other to a new level of legitimacy and security, effectively adopting, and then replacing these preceding systems to rebrand and intensify the othering of the 'criminal'. If we seek to deconstruct the notion of the ontological other as it pertains to mass incarceration and the 'criminal', we may find limited success in addressing theological interpretations of Calvinism or in confronting racial bias; these are at best only implicitly responsible for the problem we are faced with today. Racism and salvation ontology may have set the foundation for othering, but it is presently invigorated and sustained by capitalism. In any attempts to address ontological othering in society, capitalism cannot be ignored.

Having discovered who the enemy is, the next step would be to decide how to confront it – for capitalism-induced othering is not so historically entrenched, but it is certainly enormously widespread and far-reaching in society today. Addressing this in order to deconstruct societal notions of the other, then, is complicated (and beyond the scope of this paper), but it would probably begin with greater truth, transparency, and regulation in the system. Departments of Correction would need to be more transparent with its policies and its prisons, not just for the sake of accountability in the running of prisons (a separate issue), but to allow the public to meet and understand the 'criminals' that it is so willingly surrendering for incarceration. This would also provide a counterbalancing voice to the dramatized and sensational portrayals that the public is fed with by news and entertainment industries. The policy of subcontracting out corrections (a public good) to private industries would also need to be evaluated. On a societal level, more thought on addressing social stratification and gentrification might be beneficial in combating the natural outcomes that a capitalistic and completely unregulated market economy lends itself to. These policies are by no means specific or detailed, because this is a complex problem that requires a separate study to detail how to address. However, we do know that more has to be done by the government, or by social advocacy bodies, to intervene in the unregulated market by providing information, knowledge, and education beyond what the solely profit-driven free market allocates and provides. Capitalism is a good thing, but it cannot be all that is running society and the economy -- especially the criminal justice network. To address and deconstruct the notion of the 'criminal' as the ontological other, we first have to release the grip that capitalism and capitalist ways of thinking have on our society, our prison system, and what we know of them both.

Endnotes

1   I refer here to the ontological profile, in terms of corruption and inferiority in being, not other profiles (socioeconomic, ethnic, etc.) in which the profiles of the 'criminals' do differ from the rest of society, as will be discussed further on.

2   Whether the low education levels give rise to the high rates of incarceration or vice versa is a significant phenomenon that is important to address, but that is unfortunately outside the scope of this paper -- in either direction of causation, it is nevertheless undeniable that there is a clear correlation.

3   The invisible hand is the self-regulating and non-biased regulator of the market, that distributes resources according to efficiency and productivity as defined by society's demand and supply forces.

Works Cited

Adams, Susan. "Depressed At Work? You're Not Alone." *Forbes*. Forbes
Magazine, 24 July 2013. Web. 23 Apr. 2014.
<http://www.forbes.com/sites/susanadams/2013/07/24/depressed-
atwork- youre-not-alone/>.

Alexander, Michelle. *The New Jim Crow: Mass Incarceration in the Age of
Colorblindness*. New York: New, 2010. Print.

Dyer, Joel. *The Perpetual Prisoner Machine: How America Profits from
Crime*. Boulder, Colo: Westview, 2000. Print.

Foucault, Michel. *Discipline and Punish: The Birth of the Prison*. Trans.
Alan Sheridan. New York: Random House, 1979. Print.

Forman, James, Jr. "Racial Critiques Of Mass Incarceration: Beyond The
New Jim Crow." New York University Law Review 87 (2012): 101-
146. Print.

Goldman, Ivan G. *Sick Justice: Inside the American Gulag*. Dulles, VA:
Potomac, 2013. Print. Kyckelhahn, Tracey. "Bureau of Justice Statistics
(BJS) - Justice Expenditure and Employment Extracts, 2007." Bureau of
Justice Statistics (BJS). N.p., 20 Sept. 2010. Web. 24 Apr. 2014.
<http://www.bjs.gov/index.cfm?ty=pbdetail&iid=2315>.

Parenti, Christian. *Lockdown America*. London: Verso, 2008. Print.

Prins, Nomi. "Millions in the Slammer: We Must Reverse America's Zeal to
Incarcerate." *Alternet*. The Women's International Perspective, 30 Dec.
2007. Web. 23 Apr. 2014.

<http://www.alternet.org/story/72031/millions_in_the_slammer%253A_
we_must_reverse_america%27s_zeal_to_incarcerate>.

Snyder, T. Richard. *The Protestant Ethic and the Spirit of Punishment.*
Grand Rapids, MI: W.B. Eerdmans, 2001. Print.

Taylor, Mark L. *The Executed God: The Way of the Cross in Lockdown
America.* Minneapolis, MN: Fortress, 2001. Print.

Western, Bruce, and Becky Pettit. "Incarceration & Social Inequality."
Daedalus 139.3 (2010): 8-19. Print.

Yousman, Bill. *Prime Time Prisons on U.S. Tv: Representation of
Incarceration.* New York, NY: Peter Lang, 2009. Print.

Mandatory Return: Determinate Sentencing and Its Impact on Recidivism

James P. Keown, Jr.

Introduction

Governor Deval Patrick recently set an ambitious goal to reduce recidivism in Massachusetts by 50 percent over five years. The governor is leading an effort to concentrate resources on individuals considered to be at high risk to recidivate, expand rehabilitative programming inside prisons, and increase the use of minimum security facilities in an effort to improve the likelihood of a successful transition by those incarcerated back into the free world.[1] Patrick notes, "preparation for re-entry must be intentional and start at the point of entry."[2] In other words, the governor believes, to reduce recidivism, the reentry process needs to begin as soon as a person enters prison.

Professor and author, T. Richard Snyder, however, argues that recidivism "is a predictable result" of retributive criminal justice practices.[3] Unfortunately, by starting at the point of entry into the prison system, the governor focuses his reforms on prison policy and does not address the overall retributive nature of the Massachusetts criminal justice system. Specifically, he fails to account for the impact that the state's increasingly restrictive sentencing policies, such as mandatory minimum drug laws, the three strikes law, and life without parole, have on the ability for men and women to successfully transition from prison into general society.

Therefore, in light of Patrick and Snyder's ideas, this paper asks, does the retributive practice of determinate sentencing lead to increased recidivism in Massachusetts? Utilizing data from the Massachusetts Department of Correction, reports from the Pew Center on the States and MassInc., and writings by Snyder, Peter Moskos, Michel Foucault, Lawrence Friedman, Michelle Alexander, James Forman, Jr. and others, it is argued that if the Commonwealth hopes to significantly decrease recidivism, it must include sentencing reform and not simply prison reform. Such a transition requires that the current sentencing scheme centered on punishment, rather than rehabilitation, be abandoned if the Commonwealth hopes to achieve its goal of reducing the number of people returning to prison.

Recidivism

Recidivist is the technical term for those who are commonly labeled as repeat offenders. Recidivism, generally, occurs anytime a person who served a criminal sentence returns to jail or prison. Across the states, there are slight variations to what does and does not qualify as recidivism. In Massachusetts, a recidivist is defined by the state as, "any criminally sentenced inmate released to the street from [Massachusetts Department of Correction (MADOC)] jurisdiction who is reincarcerated in a Massachusetts state or county facility or a federal facility for a criminal sentence within three years of their release to the street."[4] The MADOC's Office of Strategic Planning and Research is charged with tracking recidivism and regularly reporting its findings. The numbers are not very good.

The most recent report on recidivism in Massachusetts shows that 43 percent of people released from state prisons returned in less than three years. According to the Pew Center on the States, the rate increases to approximately 60 percent when measured over a six year period versus the standard three year evaluation.[6] While many states experienced a recidivism rate of 50 percent or higher over the same time period, several concerning trends emerge from the Commonwealth's data. The most notable fact is that there was a significant increase in recidivism during the studied years. The Pew research shows that "Massachusetts was one of only eight states that had an increase of over 10 percent."[7] In fact, of the 33 states participating in the Pew study, over half reported reductions in recidivism averaging 9 percent.[8] This dramatic rise in recidivism comes after Massachusetts spent nearly 25 years expanding both what it considers a crime and what the punishment is for violating the law.

Gordon Haas is chairman of the Lifers Group at MCI-Norfolk, a prison in Massachusetts. Over the years, he has seen a staggering number of people rejoin the free world, only to return to prison in short order. Many returned on minor technical violations, which Haas says, "occur when released inmates violate a condition of parole or probation."[9] Sometimes this violation can be as simple as a parolee unable to find employment. Others return after committing new crimes. How is it that while most states are reducing recidivism, the rate in Massachusetts continues to climb? The bigger question to Haas is how can a system that allows this to occur go unchanged for so long? He likes to equate the problem to the business world. Imagine a company that saw 50 percent or more of its products returned every year. Haas says, "No corporation could remain in business with such a dismal record."[10] Former Massachusetts Correction Commissioner Michael V. Fair admitted as much when he asked, "Why do we have to publish a recidivism study every year? After all, General Motors does not take out ads bragging about their cars that are recalled."[11] Yet, not only does the Massachusetts criminal justice system remain "in business," but in many ways it continues to expand at an unprecedented pace.

Retributive Justice

Stanford Law Professor Lawrence Friedman describes criminal justice as "a particular kind of reaction to crime."[12] Much like the overall American criminal justice system. The Commonwealth operates primarily under retributive justice -- the notion that punishment is the most effective deterrent to crime. It is a concept best traced to the 1764 writing, *Essays on Crime and Punishment*.[13] In the text, Italian politician Cesare Beccaria lays out his theory of crime and punishment. Beccaria believed, "When crime paid less... there would be fewer criminals."[14] Criminal justice professor Peter Moskos describes Beccarian justice as, "swift, certain, and proportional to the crime."[15] As the United States was founded, these ideas on justice were seen as reforms. The will of the English monarch was replaced by the will of the American people, enforced by laws and punishment, creating a new system believed to be "more rational, more modern, more just and humane."[16] The system, however, promoted a separation in society. On one side stood the "Us" of citizens. On the other side stood the "Them" of criminals. In *Crime and Punishment in American History*, Friedman writes, "criminal law was (and is) part of the official process of labeling and identifying who is in and who is out, who is deviant and who is mainstream."[17] Through this act of labeling, retribution moves to the center of the American criminal justice system.

Retributive justice declares, "The problem is 'Them' not 'Us'. Blame takes precedence over responsibility and punishment becomes the only conceivable means of correction. Therefore, when a crime is committed, there is a cry for justice, which to many is synonymous with revenge. In a modern society, however, personal vengeance -- outside the world of television and movies -- is taboo. So the state steps in, often with the same vindictive spirit of revenge that desires punishment above all else.[18] Crime is considered a societal issue, but criminal acts are treated as isolated individual incidents. In Massachusetts, for example, a defendant might be able to use the fact that she is poor, unemployed, from a broken home, or addicted to drugs to speak to her state of mind at the time of committing a crime, but none of these things are considered a viable defense in court. No, the will of the people and their spirit of vengeance says, "She did the crime -- now, she needs to do the time." That said, retribution has not always been seen as the answer to crime.

Reform Attempts

While for most of the past two centuries, America held onto the belief that fast and firm punishment is both the best reaction to crime and the best way to prevent crime, attempts were made to move away from a criminal justice system built on retribution, in favor of more rehabilitative models. The most recent push took shape in the early 1960s when "most Americans held the optimistic view that offenders could be reformed and that it was the responsibility of the criminal justice system to do so."[19] Prisons focused on treatment and programs designed to help men and women overcome the litany of issues that led them to prison, such as drug abuse and a lack of education.

Correction policies in Massachusetts followed the national trend and shifted away from punishment towards rehabilitation through the 1960s and 1970s.[20] One of the hallmarks of this period was the flexibility judges in the Commonwealth had in determining the length of sentences imposed on those convicted of crimes. Courts had the ability to take into account all the facts related to a case when handing down a sentence. In addition, the length of a sentence was often crafted in a manner that empowered correction officials to release individuals they deemed ready to successfully return to the free world.[21] During this time, Massachusetts prisons housed considerable fewer men and women compared to today and diligently worked to rehabilitate those who were incarcerated. In fact, according to a 2013 MassInc. report, "Massachusetts was highly regarded for developing innovative programs to reduce recidivism, as well as its work evaluating these programs with the strongest research methods available at the time."[22] The rehabilitative reform movement in Massachusetts, however, did not last long.

Return to Retribution

In the mid-1970s, a series of studies were published calling into question the effectiveness of rehabilitative programming. One such study by Robert Martinson came to the simple conclusion that "nothing works" in rehabilitating men and women in prison.[23] These studies coincided with a rise in crime both in Massachusetts and around the country that continued into the 1980s and 1990s. The Commonwealth quickly retreated to the old practice of punishment and abandoned many of its progressive rehabilitation strategies.

Starting in the 1980s, Massachusetts, along with many other states and the federal government, engaged in the "Tough on Crime" criminal justice movement. The once celebrated reforms of the Commonwealth were now held out as examples of how not to respond to crime. Governor Michael Dukakis was portrayed by conservatives as the preeminent "soft on crime" politician during his 1988 presidential bid. The now infamous Willie Horton campaign advertisement crystallized in many people's minds that punishment was the only answer.

Determinate Sentencing

A series of policy changes ushered in the new era of retributive justice. As Princeton sociologist Devah Pager notes, "One of the most influential changes to the system concerned sentencing policies."[24] As America shifted back towards punishment-centric practices, both the federal and state government passed measures to create determinate, or mandatory, sentences. In Massachusetts, Governor Dukakis signed into law a mandatory minimum drug law in 1988. It was quickly followed by laws that significantly increased the sentences of drug offenses committed near schools, parks, and playgrounds, and another mandatory minimum drug bill specifically targeting drug dealers.[25]

Determinate sentencing, coupled with "truth in sentencing", which required a person to serve at least 85 percent of their sentence before being eligible for release, created an environment where millions of people who in the past would have received probation at most, now found themselves in prison." The chances of receiving a prison sentence following arrest increased by more than 50 percent as a result of determinate sentencing laws," Pager writes.[26] Not only did more people find themselves incarcerated, but due to harsher penalties and truth in sentencing, they found themselves locked up for longer periods of time.

250 years after Beccaria established his retributive principles, there are approximately 2.3 million people incarcerated in the United States. That figure equates to more than 1 in 100 adults locked up nationwide.[27] To envision the sheer scale of American mass incarceration, think about it how Moskos does. "If we condensed our nationwide penal system into a single city, it would be the fourth largest city in America, with a population greater than Baltimore, Boston and San Francisco combined."[28] In Massachusetts, the percentage of the population sentenced to prison has tripled since the 1980s.[29] There are some who examine the current incarceration numbers and attempt to make a "chicken and egg" argument. Such people claim the unprecedented jump in those sent to prison is not because of changes in the law, but rather because of changes in crime rates which necessitated new laws. Michelle Alexander in The New Jim Crow argues otherwise. She points to a report by Marc Mauer which "suggests that the entire increase in the prison population from 1980 to 2001 can be explained by sentencing policy changes."[30] Yale Law Professor James Forman, Jr. echoing Alexander's contentions, writes in the New York University Law Review, "We divert fewer offenders than we once did, send more of them to prison, and keep them in prison longer."[31]

If there was any question as to whether retributive justice had returned to Massachusetts, Governor William Weld removed all doubt. At a 1992 Summit on Corrections, he stated, "we have to undo many years in which Massachusetts treated crime as a social services matter."[32] When discussing the Commonwealth's brief experimentation with rehabilitation, the governor lamented, "There was an unfortunate lack of punishment."[33] The state's primary determinate sentencing policies: mandatory minimum drug laws, the three strikes law, and life without parole, represent "a spirit of punishment." Snyder says, such a spirit, "makes us quick to judge, quick to imagine the worst, quick to desire retribution and vengeance."[37] Each law also has specific implications on how many people return to prison in Massachusetts each year.

Mandatory Minimum Drug Laws

Sentencing practices that include a mandatory number of years, set by statute, a person must serve in prison before being eligible for release have a long history in America. The first such mandatory minimum law, for treason, was enacted in 1790. But the practice of setting determinate sentences was all but relegated to obscurity until the federal Boggs Act in 1951 began applying mandatory minimums to drug crimes.[38] The laws demonstrated little effectiveness, and by 1970, most were repealed by Congress.

In the 1980s, as the retributive criminal justice model reemerged, America declared a war on Drugs. One tactic the government used to wage its war was a return to mandatory minimums. Following passage of the Anti Drug Abuse Act in 1986, the U.S. prison population exploded, Massachusetts, following the national trend, experienced a similar increase in those sent to prison because of new mandatory minimum statutes. In 1985, drug offenders comprised only 6 percent of the MADOC population.[39] Five years later, following passage of the state's new determinate sentencing policies, 20 percent of all inmates were serving time for a drug offense.[40]

Today, approximately 22 percent of the Commonwealth's prison population is made up of drug offenders -- 70 percent of whom were sentenced under one of the state's 31 mandatory minimum laws.[41]

As early as 1995, Massachusetts acknowledged there were serious problems with determinate sentencing. In the fall of that year, state legislators commissioned a panel to study the policies in the wake of a *Boston Globe* series that exposed serious flaws in the system.[42] The commission determined mandatory minimums do not deter drug crimes and actually inhibit justice. "There can be no justice in our courts," the panel wrote, "if a Judge is prohibited from sitting in judgement."[43] The report concluded, "Anything which hinders a judge's efforts to fulfill those obligations provides a disservice not only to the courts and the criminal justice system but to the Commonwealth's citizenry as well."[44]

Nearly 20 years after the state's legislative panel recommended eliminating mandatory minimum drug laws, Massachusetts still holds onto vestiges of the failed statutes. A report by MassInc. and Community Resources for Justice reaffirmed that the state's practice of "incarcerating greater numbers of drug offenders produces very small decreases in crime."[45] In 2012, reformers led by the group Families Against Mandatory Minimums successfully lobbied for changes to the state's drug laws. The measure did not eliminate determinate drug sentencing, but it reduced the severity of the punishment assessed to those convicted of drug offenses. As a result, hundreds of people serving time in Massachusetts qualified for earlier transitions to minimum security facilities and earlier release.

Lost in the celebration of finally beginning the process of dismantling the Commonwealth's ineffective drug statutes was the fact that success came at a price. As the drug bill advanced towards final passage, a high-profile murder gripped Massachusetts residents. Dominic Cenelli, recently paroled from a habitual offender life sentence, shot and killed a Woburn, Massachusetts police officer while attempting to flee after an armed robbery at a department store. Even though Cenelli was also killed in the shoot-out, the public's spirit of vengeance demanded retribution. It would come as an attachment to the new drug bill, and it would guarantee that certain repeat offenders would have little chance of reentering the free world, regardless of circumstances.

Three Strikes Law

The story of Lester Wallace is one of the most important lessons in America's embrace of retributive justice over the past 25 years. Early in the morning of March 8, 1994, Wallace, "a homeless schizophrenic," broke into a car and tried to steal the car's radio.[46] Within moments, he was caught, booked, and charged. Little did Wallace realize, he was about to become the first victim of California's Proposition 184 -- better known as, "The Three Strikes Law." The measure, which sent a person to prison for 25 years to life if convicted of any crime after two previous felony convictions had gone into effect just nine hours earlier.[43] Matt Taibbi examines the history of California's Three Strikes Law and the impact it had on America:

> The overwhelming support for the measure [72 percent of California voters supported Proposition 184] touched off a nationwide get-tough on-crime movement, embraced especially by third-way Democrats, who seized upon the policy idea as a powerful weapon in their efforts to throw off their party's bleeding-heart image and recapture the political center.[48]

In less than five years, nearly half the country and the federal government had a version of Three Strikes in place. "Not all are as harsh as the

California law," Taibbi says, "but they all embrace the basic principle of throw-away-the-key mandatory sentencing for the incorrigible recidivist."[49]

Two decades later, California officials -- including tough on crime conservatives -- have come to the conclusion that Three Strikes simply does not work. Even some of the toughest of the tough, such as former Los Angeles and current New York police chief William Bratton conclude the policy fails to achieve its goals. Bratton admits a Three Strikes policy "has political appeal for dealing with repeat offenders," however, "Evidence has shown limited impact on crime levels."[51] In fact, as Mark Arnold notes in the *Bakersfield Californian*, "Non-three strikes states had a violent crime rate that was 29.5 percent lower than Califonia's."[52]

The failures of California echo across the country in each state that took a similar Three Strikes approach. Yet, with twenty years of data pointing to the total ineffectiveness of Three Strikes, Massachusetts passed a version of the law in August 2012. Under the Commonwealth's version of the law, a person must receive a sentence of 15-25 years to life if convicted of any felony deemed "serious" by the state, if the person already has two previous felony convictions.

Why did Massachusetts wait almost 20 years to join the league of Three Strikes states? It seemed the best option to Governor Patrick and the state legislature who were besieged in 2012 with cries to make laws tougher on repeat offenders after the aforementioned incident involving Cenelli. Instead of reviewing the scores of data on how Three Strikes fails to live up to its promises, Massachusetts merely reacted and did its best to look tough -- like so many states before.

While the Commonwealth's Three Strikes law is too new to produce quantifiable data, predictions to what the outcomes might be can be made. In Massachusetts, an analogous group exist -- lifers not convicted of murder. A number of crimes already qualify for a sentence of life with the possibility of parole (15 years to life or 15-25 years to life -- depending on the date of the crime). There are approximately 900 individuals currently serving a second degree life sentence in Massachusetts.[53] Of them, nearly 100 are non-murder convictions.[54] In 2013, 12 percent of the lifers who went before the parole board fell into this category.[55] Only three received parole.[56] Once labeled as a "lifer," regardless of crime, the chances of ever being released in Massachusetts diminish greatly.

Author and Northeastern Professor James Alan Fox notes, "it is much too tempting to embrace the frightening notion that paroled lifers are indeed at high risk for committing serious crimes once released back to the community."[57] The numbers tell a different story. More than half of paroled lifers who returned to prison are reincarcerated for technical violations and not new offenses. Those who do commit new crimes, as Fox notes, "typically engaged in activity that was far less injurious than that which landed them in prison in the first place."[59] But when a spirit of vengeance motivates policy decisions, facts rarely matter. Retributive justice demands that life means life.

Life Without Parole

Early in 2012, Republican Mississippi Governor Haley Barbour launched a political firestorm when he released 198 people from prison -- four of whom had been convicted of murder.[60] In the backlash that followed the move, those opposed to the governor's leniency pointed to the four individuals serving life without parole (LWOP) as examples of Barbour subverting both the law and the will of the people. The state Supreme Court upheld the governor's decision, but Mississippi politicians quickly jockeyed to reassure the public that they had not gone soft on crime.[61]

Life without parole, as the name suggests, is a terminal sentence handed down on those, generally, but not exclusively, found guilty of murder. In 16 states and the federal system, LWOP is utilized as a mandatory minimum in murder convictions.[62] Massachusetts also uses LWOP as a mandatory sentence for anyone convicted of first-degree murder -- defined as premeditated and particularly cruel or atrocious. In addition, the Commonwealth may impose LWOP on anyone "convicted as joint ventures or co-conspirators in a crime in which someone else took a human life with or without prior intent."[63] In such cases, it is not uncommon for the person "most culpable in the crime" to one day leave prison, while those considered co-defendants are forced to spend the rest of their lives incarcerated.[64]

Since 1992, there has been a 300 percent increase in the use of LWOP in the United States.[65] Massachusetts has experienced a 188 percent increase in LWOP sentences from 1990 to today.[66] If one looks backs to the 1970s, when LWOP first began expanding, the changes are even more considerable. In 1977, there were 170 people in Massachusetts serving LWOP, compared to more than 1,000 today -- an increase of over 550 percent.[67]

As more states turn away from the death penalty LWOP is seen as a more humane alternative. Those sentenced to LWOP are deemed unfit by the criminal justice system to live in the free world. In lieu of an execution, people are locked away, often for decades, until they die in prison. Where the sentence fails, according to Lloyd Fillion of the Criminal Justice Policy Coalition, is that "LWOP ignores the obvious fact that over time some prisoners no longer pose a threat to harm others."[69]

In fact, those sentenced to LWOP may actually be the least likely group of convicted persons to recidivate. According to a study by The Sentencing Project, 79.4 percent of lifers released nationwide in 1994 remained out of prison in the three year period following their release -- more than double the rate of the entire released population.[70] Individual states demonstrate comparable trends. "As of 2008, not one of 440 murderers and attempted murderers, released in New York from 2004 through 2007, has been returned to prison for a new crime."[71] Similar numbers are seen in Massachusetts. "While the state does not collect risk assessment data for first-degree lifers," states a 2013 MassInc. report, "data on second-degree lifers show that they are the least likely to reoffend."[72]

A current effort is underway to reform LWOP, along with other mandatory sentences. Among the most vocal groups in the initiative are judges. Often frustrated by the lack of discretion at their disposal, judges regularly express dissatisfaction during sentencing hearings for the terms they are forced to impose. In one such instance, a judge noted, "had he not been forced to issue an LWOP sentence, he would have opted for a term of ten to twelve years."[73]

The justices of the United States Supreme Court added their voices to the debate on LWOP when, in June 2012, they issued their decision in Miller v. Alabama. The Court in Miller held that those who were juveniles at the time of their crime, could not receive a mandatory sentence of life in prison without the possibility of parole.[74] The decision touched off a nationwide review of LWOP statutes that is ongoing.

In the face of all the data related to LWOP, there is still a spirit of vengeance at work. Kent Scheidegger, legal director of the Criminal Justice Legal Foundation believes those convicted of murder should receive LWOP or death. He says, "If they've gotten life without parole, they've gotten off easy."[75] Those who believe as Scheidegger does, fail not only to understand the complexities of sentencing men and women to life, but the negative impact all mandatory sentencing has on the success of the criminal justice system.

Realities of Mandatory Sentencing

There are several contentions one can make against the effectiveness of mandatory sentencing. Recently, the primary point used by reformers is that determinate sentencing is a costly solution that offers a poor return on investment. While such an argument may gain traction with conservatives who are fiscally conscious but tough on crime, it fails to properly express the larger defects in the system. Mandatory sentencing sends more people to prison for longer periods of time, while providing them with less resources to successfully live in the free world. The policies do this while targeting, above all else, women and people of color. And, in the end, the practice helps guarantee that nearly 50 percent of individuals released from prison will return in less than three years.

More People Less Resources

As more men and women fill Massachusetts prisons, there are far fewer resources to assist in preparing for reentry. Since 1990, 60 percent of the growth in the MADOC population came from LWOP and mandatory minimum drug sentences.[76] These two categories continue to tax the corrections system to a breaking point. Today, Massachusetts residents dole out more than 500 million dollars annually to fund state prisons (and another 300 million dollars for county jails).[77] Over the last five years, however, the only line in the MADOC budget to decrease every year was rehabilitative programming.[78]A meager 2.2 percent of the correction budget in fiscal year 2013 was allocated to provide education, job training, addiction assistance, and other programming to those incarcerated.[79] Instead, the bulk of the budget, approximately 60 percent, went to administrative and security staff.

The lack of available resources recently forced the department to enact a new policy which excludes large groups of the MADOC population from certain programs, such as vocational education and drug and alcohol recovery. Using a computer program called COMPAS, everyone who enters a Massachusetts prison is labeled either low-risk or high-risk based on a series of factors. High-risk labeled individuals with the least amount of time to serve, then, are offered access to programs. Those labeled low-risk or with longer sentences are forced to wait and hope a program spot opens. Lifers, because they have no sentence wrap-up date, are all but excluded from certain programs.

A report by the MADOC, produced in conjunction with the Urban Institute, reported that only 27 percent of those who recidivated during the study period received any vocational or job training while in prison.[81] The report goes on to reveal, "46 percent said that they had wanted to participate in such training but had been unable to do so."[82] Because of the over-populating of Massachusetts prisons by determinate sentences, the MADOC is forced to triage those who desire rehabilitative programming.

The result is that more men and women leave prison with little or no assistance in overcoming the hurdles that originally led to their incarceration.

Vengeful Equity

The particular challenges women face returning to the free world often get lost in reentry discussions. One modern trend in American's retributive criminal justice system is the idea of "vengenful equity."[83] Meda Chesney-Lind describes the term as the system's ability to treat women just as poorly as men. A leading instrument in administering vengeful equity is determinate sentencing. During the 1990s, while crimes committed by women increased by only 14.5 percent, the number of women sent to prison jumped by 105.8 percent.[84] The rise was led by the scores of women caught in the net of mandatory minimum drug laws. As violent offenses by women declined from 48.9 percent of the incarcerated population in 1979 to 28.5 percent in 1998, those serving time for drug crimes rapidly grew.[85] By 1998, one in three women in U.S. prisons were there because of drug laws.[86] Massachusetts, again, conforms to the national trend. Since 1980, the number of women sentenced to prison in the Commonwealth has nearly tripled.[87] Determinate sentencing did not simply send more women to prison, it sent entirely new groups there. A study by Human Rights Watch of women in New York found that of those locked up after mandatory minimums were enacted, "nearly half (44 percent) had never been in prison before, and 17 percent had never been arrested before."[88]

Incarceration, especially long mandatory sentences, affect women differently from men. Karen Heimer believes that the societal realities of family composition and wage inequality accentuate the difficulties women face reentering the free world.[89] Heimer asserts that women are increasingly serving as the head of single-parent households, especially in poorer communities, but are economic afterthoughts in the workplace.[90] When compounded by a criminal record that both limits employment opportunities and establishes a layer of state vigilance over how children are raised, successfully navigating the free world for many women is simply impossible. Add to these factors the reality that many women leaving prison also no longer qualify for welfare, public housing, and other federal and state assistance. Heimer, therefore, concludes, the outcome of mandatory sentencing "encourages economically marginalized girls and women (particularly those who have already been convicted of crimes) to seek to survive through crime."[91]

Minorities

Incarceration policies, such as determinate sentences, disproportionately impact minorities. African-Americans in Massachusetts are incarcerated at a rate eight times higher than white residents. For Latinos, the rate is six times higher than whites.[92] Michelle Alexander has cast a strong spotlight on how America's tough on crime agenda has captured an unbalanced proportion of people of color. As she writes in *The New Jim Crow*, minorities leaving prison live under a system barely distinguishable from the one used to discriminate against African-Americans in the post-Reconstruction South. Alexander says, "Today a criminal freed from prison has scarcely more rights, and arguably less respect, than a freed slave or a black person living 'free' in Mississippi at the height of Jim Crow."[93]

While Alexander confines her argument mainly to the War on Drugs, racial disparity exists across all versions of determinate sentencing in

Massachusetts. For people of color, mandatory sentencing policies do not simply send more people of color to prison, they also help guarantee one in two will return in less than three years.[94] A 2014 report on recidivism in Massachusetts revealed that African-Americans represented 25 percent of those released from prison, but 28 percent of those who recidivated.[95] While four out of ten whites and Latinos returned to prison, nearly half of all African-Americans were reincarcerated in less than 36 months.[96] More than any other race, African-Americans bear the greatest burden of mandatory sentencing. As Alexander articulates, "Once labeled a felon, the badge of inferiority remains with you for the rest of your life, relegating you to a permanent second-class status. "[97]

Prison Label

The prison label placed upon men and women returning to the free world goes beyond the outward forces writers such as Alexander describe. It is also important to note the psychological impact mandatory sentences have on people. Several studies point to the negative consequences lengthy determinate sentences have on those seeking to return to the free world. One study on extended incarceration by Craig Haney at the University of California, Santa Cruz notes, how such sentences, "may interfere with the transition from prison to home, impede an ex-convict's successful re-intergration into a social network and employment setting, and may compromise an incarcerated parent's ability to resume his or her role with family and children."[98] These effects are exasperated when a person is unable to shed the prison label. Such situations are, "likely to doom most social and intimate relations."[99] The long, unforgiving sentences handed down as required through determinate states do not only affix labels to men and women, but can psychologically scar them as well. Is it any wonder than, that so many individuals so often gravitate back toward the physical prison of incarceration than remain in the invisible prison of the, so-called, free world.

Conclusion

When examining recidivism, both what leads to it and how to reduce it, falling into a numbers trap is easy. For example, if Governor Patrick desires to reduce recidivism by 50 percent, one could argue that he need only commute the sentences for all those serving life without parole and offer them parole. Besides not being politically realistic, such solutions fail to address the mitigating factors that lead to recidivism. The same can be said for the governor's current plan to lower recidivism through prison reform. Without addressing the number of people in prison, the length of time they are there, and the unique barriers standing between each person and successful reentry, almost any plan will fail to meet the governor's lofty goals.

After a quarter century, it should be clear that determinate sentencing is failing Massachusetts. While the retributive practice has locked up more men and women than ever before, it has done little to truly help those returning to the free world succeed at staying out of prison. In actuality, as MassInc. determined, mandatory sentencing, "increases the likelihood they will engage in further criminal activity."[100]

The spirit of vengeance driving determinate sentencing is slowly starting to dissipate in Massachusetts. According to a 2014 poll of state residents, 59 percent believe a person released from a Massachusetts prison is more "likely to commit new crime because they've been hardened by their experience."[101] Whereas in the past, such a feeling led to cries for more punishment, those polled overwhelmingly expressed a much different desire. 43 percent want a stronger emphasis on crime prevention and 21 percent want an emphasis on rehabilitation. Only 15 percent, in contrast, think punishment is still the best solution.[102] The most notable numbers may well be that 67 percent of those polled say, "reform the system so fewer people are sent to prison," and 85 percent call for a return to discretionary sentencing by judges. The will of the people appears to have moved away from retribution and determinate sentencing. Now the people, especially those currently and once incarcerated, must wait to see how long it takes for the criminal justice system in Massachusetts to do the same.

Endnotes

1. Patrick, Deval. "Governor Patrick Outlines Series of Reforms to Reduce Recidivism by 50 Percent Over the Next Five Years." Commonwealth of Massachusetts. Office of the Governor. 20 February 2014(accessed 22 Feb 2014). Online. www.mass.gov
2. ibid.
3. Snyder, T. Richard The Protestant Ethic and the Spirit of Punishment Grand Rapids:, 2001. Print (72)
4. Kohl, Rhiana, Ph. D. with Ashle Montgomery and Hollie Matthews. Recidivism Rates of 2007 Release Cohort. Massachusetts Department of Correction: April 2012. Print.
5. ibid.
6. Pew Center on the States. State of Recidivism: The Revolving Door of America's Prisons. The Pew Charitable Trust. Washington, D.C. April 2011. Print.
7. Forman, Benjamin and John Larivee. Crime, Cost, and Consequences Is It Time to Get Smart on Crime? Boston: Mass Inc. And Community Resources For Justice, March 2013. (20)
8. ibid.
9. Haas, Gordon. Recidivism end the Massachusetts Department of Corrections: A Report on Recidivism Rates for 1998 and 2007 Norfolk: Lifers Group, 2014. Print.
10. ibid.
11. Testimony of Dr. Michael W. Forcier Regarding the Need for a Department of Correction Advisory Board. Massachusetts State Legislature. 15 March 2001. Print.
12. Friedman, Lawrence M. Crime and Punishmert in American. New York Basic, 1993. (8)
13. Moskos, Peter. In Defense of Flogging. New York: Basic, 2011.
14. ibid
15. ibid
16. Foucalt, Michel. Discipline & Punish The Birth of Prison. New York: Vantage Books, 1977, 1995. (63)
17. Friedman. (84)
18. Snyder. (45)
19. Pager, Devah. Marked- Race, Crime and Finding Work in an Era of Mass Incarceration. Chicago: Univ. of Chicago, 2009. (15)
20. Forman – MassInc. (10)
21. ibid.
22 ibid.
23. Pager. (15)

24. ibid (16)

25. Forman. (10)

26. Pager. (17)

27. Henrichsen, Christian and Ruth Delaney. The Price of Prisons: What Incarceration Costs Taxpayers. NewYork: VERA Institute of Justice, 2012. (2)

28. Moskos (14)

29. Forman - Massinc. (10)

30. Alexander, Michelle. The New Jim Crow - Mass Incarceration in the Age of Colorblindness.New York: New Press, 2012. Print. (93)

31. Forman. James, Jr. "Racial Critiques of Mass Incarceration: Beyond the New Jim Crow New York University Law Review. Vol 87 (2012): 101-146. Print. (126)

32. Weld, William F. "Remarks by Governor William F. Weld: The Attorney General's Summit on Corrections: Commonwealth of Massachusetts. Office of the Governor. April 1992. Print.

33. ibid.

37. Snyder. (44)
Massachusetts. According to a 2014 poll of state residents, 59 percent believe a person released from a Massachusetts

38. Gips, Michael. "Run-On Sentencing - Mandatory Minimum Sentencing, a Proven Failure, May Soon Be Expanded." The District. 19 November 1993 (accessed 18 March 2014). Online. www.washingtoncitypaper.com

39. Forman - Masslnc. (16)

40.ibid.

41. ibid.

42. NDSN. "Massachusetts Panel Reviews Mandatory Minimum Sentencing, Issues Strong Report and Legislation." December 1995(accessed18 March 2014). Online www.ndsn.org

43. ibid.

44. ibid.

45. Forman - Masslnc. (15) .

46. Taibbi, Matt. "Cruel and Unusual Punishment: The Shame of Three Strikes Law." The Movement Winter 2013. Print.

47. ibid. (39)

48. ibid. (38)

49. ibid. (41)

50. ibid. (41)

51. ibid.

52. Arnold, Mark. "California's three-strike law is a costly failure that does little to reduce crime and more to increase taxpayers' cost for

incarcerating aging and non-violent criminals." Bakersfield Californian. 9 February 2006(accessed18 March 2014). Online. www.bakersfieldcalifomian.com.

53. Haas, Gordon. A Report on the Massachusetts Department of Correction - 2011. Norfolk: Lifers Group, 2012. Print.

54. ibid.

55. Haas, Gordon. Parole Decisions 2013. Norfolk: Lifers Group. (16)

56. ibid.

57. Fox, James Alan. "Parole failure - Glass 1/3 empty or 2/3 full?" Corrections.com. July 2011 (Accessed 18 March 2014). Online. www.corrections.com

58. ibid.

59. ibid.

60. Nellis, Ashley. "Tinkering with Life: A Look at the inappropriateness of Life without Parole as an Alternative to the Death Penalty." University of Miami Law Review. Vol OT (2013). 439-458.Print. (446)

61. ibid. (446)

62. ibid. (441)

63. Fillion, Lloyd and Gordon Haas. Life without Parole - A Reconsideration. Norfolk: Lifers Group, 2010. Print (4)

64. ibid.

65. Nellis. (446)

66. Forman - Masslnc. (15)

67. Fillion (2)

68. Nellis (441)

69. Fillion (3)

70. ibid. (17)

71. ibid.

72. Forman - MassInc. (15)

73. Nellis (453)

74.ibid.

75. Fillion (22)

75. Forman - MassInc. (14,15)

77. Haas, Gordon. A Report on the Massachusetts Department of Correction - 2011. Norfolk: Lifers Group, 2012. (15)

78. ibid.

79. ibid.

80. ibid.

81. Brooks, Lisa, Amy L Solomon, Rhiana Kohl, et al. Reincarcerated: The Experience of Men Returning to Massachusetts Prison. MADOC and the Urban Institute, April 2008.

82. ibid.

83. Chesney-Lind, Meda "Imprisoning Women: The Unintended Victims of Mass Imprisonment. "Invisible Punishment: The Collateral Consequences of Mass imprisonment. eds. Marc Mauer and Meda Chesney-Line. New York: The New Press, 2002. Print. (91)

84. ibid. (87)

85. ibid. (88)

86. ibid. (88)

87. ibid. (88)

88. ibid.

89. ibid. (86,87)

90. ibid. .

91. ibid.

92. Forman - Masslnc. (20)

93. Alexander. (122)

94. Haas - Recidivism.

95. ibid.

95. ibid.

97. .Alexander. (93)

98. Haney, Craig. "The Psychological Impact of incarceration: Implications for Post-Prison Adjustment." From Prison to Home: The Effect of Incarceration and Reentry on Children, Families, and Communities. The University of California, Santa Cruz. December 2001(accessed5April 2012). Online. aspc.hhs.gov

99. ibid.

100. Masslnc. Polling Group. "Ready for Reform? Public Opinion on Criminal Justice in Massachusetts." Masslnc., 2014(accessed11 March 2014). Online. www.massinc.com

101. ibid.

102. ibid.

A Vicious Cycle: The Effect of Child Abuse on Juvenile Arrest

Emily Henson

"There is no keener revelation of a society's soul than the way in which it treats its children."

--Nelson Mandela

Introduction

Every day, 4,028 children are arrested in America (Children's Defense Fund, 2014). That is one every 21 seconds. Of those children arrested, more than 70,000 are held in custody in America's juvenile detention centers or correctional facilities each year (The Sentencing Project, 2011). This amounts to 225 confined youth per 100,000 in the total youth population. To put these numbers in perspective, that is more adolescents than currently reside in mid-sized American cities like Nashville, Tennessee; Portland, Oregon; or Baltimore, Maryland. These numbers do not include the more than 500,000 juveniles put on probation—and, as such, under the purview of correctional control—each year (OJJDP Statistical Briefing Book, 2010). If these statistics are jarring, they should be: The United States incarcerates more juveniles than any other country in the world (Mendel, 2011).

Moreover, three out of every five confined youth in the United States are minorities. While African Americans constitute only 16% of the entire U.S. youth population, they make up 40% of all incarcerated youth, making African American adolescents five times more likely to be incarcerated than their white peers (The Annie E. Casey Foundation, 2013; Mendel, 2011). These disparities portend a system that indecorously treats youth of color, particularly African Americans, more punitively than white youth. This disproportionate regime of punishment is not unique to youth discipline, however, but can be understood within the larger context of what David Garland (2001) has called "mass incarceration"—the steady, precipitous climb of U.S. incarceration rates from 1975 to the present which includes the systemic imprisonment of whole groups of people, particularly a concentration in disadvantaged minority populations.

Many progressive scholars, like Michelle Alexander (2010), look at these skyrocketing numbers and their significant racial disparity and rebuke the collateral damage from America's unending war on drugs—which is targeted primarily at disadvantaged communities of color—drawing a provocative analogy between current racially discriminatory criminal justice practices and the old de jure racial segregation system of Jim Crow which overtly discriminated against individuals on the basis of their race. Other scholars, like James Forman (2012) are similarly vexed by the preponderance of evidence that bespeaks discrimination in America's justice system, but proffer another more nuanced interpretation of the origins of our collective crisis. Forman argues persuasively that the myopic focus on the drug war obfuscates much that matters and belies the complexity and many dimensions of America's current crisis of punishment. Specifically, Forman advocates for a more comprehensive understanding of mass incarceration that includes acknowledging the role violence plays in America's accelerating prison population—not merely to condemn violence, but to understand and seek to ameliorate the conditions that give rise to it. After all, Forman (2012) argues, "the same low-income young people of color who disproportionately enter prisons are disproportionately victimized by crime—the two phenomena are mutually reinforcing" (pg.50).

This is the starting point for my research. Following this line of thought which intimates a vicious cycle of violence as one element in America's incarceration crisis, I was inspired by a story Forman went on to tell about a former student of his named Bobby who had been assigned to an alternative school for teens from the juvenile court system as a result of fighting at school after being robbed and witnessing his friend get killed. In recounting his experience, Bobby's attitude disclosed a profound incredulity at the lack of accountability for such senseless violence. When asked about his experiences in school Bobby replied with a poignant and haunting question: *Why do your best when it can all be taken away from you in a mere seconds?* While there are no easy answers to these kinds of tragic situations, we must not ignore or avoid the questions they raise. Bobby's story reminds us that "tough kids" also seek safety and security and that their own acts of violence or otherwise hostile, anti-social behavior are often closely connected to being in environments that feel unsafe. Bobby's response is a plea for accountability. But that accountability need not mandate a response of punitive justice. Allowing ourselves to hear Bobby's painful story, as Foreman suggests, might instead lead us to ask what accountability really means and how can it be envisioned in a way that is life-affirming for all involved parties.

Research Outline

This project is an attempt to take seriously this question of accountability and to explore the role that environments of violence and instability play in a child's risk of being swept up into the fray of our current crisis of mass punishment. Specifically, I am interested in when an adolescent is most at risk for being arrested as a juvenile for the first time and what predicts that risk. Following the arguments put forth by Michelle Alexander (2010) and James Forman (2012), I will investigate the role of both race, and environmental violence and instability, as predictors of juvenile arrest. As detailed further below, I will operationalize the experience of an "environment of violence and instability" as whether or not an adolescent experienced abuse or neglect as a child. Both child maltreatment and juvenile arrest and incarceration are pernicious social problems with devastating consequences. By exploring the link between the two, I hope to unravel more of the complex web of America's current system of juvenile injustices.

I will conduct this research using data made available by the Data Resources Program of the National Institute of Justice (Data Resources Program, 2013). Using this data on juvenile arrests, I will conduct a statistical analysis using the method of discrete time survival analysis. I will fit a taxonomy of nested logistic regression models, first examining the effects of abuse on the risk of juvenile arrest and then examining those effects within the context of race, and the interaction between those two predictors in order to understand how the effects of abuse on the probability of juvenile arrest are mediated by an individual's race. After conducting the analysis and presenting my results, I will discuss my findings within the context of other research and prominent theories that frame the larger debate in the literature on America's incarceration epidemic.

In particular, I will look at Michele Alexander's (2010) claim that the criminal justice system is creating and perpetuating a racial hierarchy in the U.S. to assess how my findings corroborate these claims. Furthermore, I will situate my findings within the work of life-course and labeling theories which assert that being officially designated a "criminal" or "delinquent" changes the way social institutions treat individuals, resulting in cumulative disadvantages that increasingly diminish later life chances, particularly molded by school and employment opportunities, in order to explicate how the outcome of juvenile arrest further shapes inequality in America (Bernburg, Krohn, & Rivera 2006; Bernburg & Krohn, 2003; Sampson & Laub, 1997). From this framework of labeling, I will then draw on Richard Snyder's (2000) arguments against American individualized notions of sin and grace to argue for more collective responsibility to children who are at risk for getting caught in cycles of violence, thus becoming victims to the tyranny of circumstance and potentially suffering further harmful consequences beyond the act(s) of abuse itself.

Background

Over the past thirty years, social scientific research has identified important links between early physical abuse and numerous poor developmental outcomes, including later violent behavior and delinquency (Ireland, Smith & Thornberry, 2002; Stouthamer-Loeber, 2001; Fergusson & Lynskey, 1997; Widom, 1989). For example, using a prospective cohort design, Widom (1989) found that individuals who experienced abuse or neglect as a child were 36% more likely than non-abused individuals to have an adult criminal record for a violent crime. Stouthamer-Loeber (2001) reported that boys with a history of abuse or neglect were more likely to display overt disruptive delinquent behaviors and experience conflicts with police authorities through late adolescence than were boys who had not been maltreated. Similarly, using data from the Rochester Youth Development Study, Thornberry and his colleagues (Ireland, Smith & Thornberry, 2002) have found that substantiated abuse or neglect is related to delinquency and drug use when adolescents are 14 to 18 years old. Moreover, other studies have established links between early physical abuse and subsequent negative social and psychological problems, including internalizing mental health problems such as depression and anxiety (Rogosch, Cicchetti, & Aber, 1995), and decreased academic performance and educational attainment (Lansford et al., 2002). In sum, findings from a number of studies support the vicious cycle hypothesis intimated by Forman's arguments that suggest that childhood histories of instability, characterized here by childhood abuse or neglect, predispose the individual to violent or antisocial behavior in later years.

Furthermore, a substantial body of research exists linking the outcome of juvenile arrest to diminished life opportunities and negative life outcomes. For example, Bernburg & Krohn (2003) found that police interaction, in the form of juvenile arrest, decreases the odds of high school graduation by over 70%. Sweeten (2006) found that a first arrest in high school nearly doubles the likelihood of dropping out. For arrested juveniles who do manage to graduate, policies denying educational benefits to individuals with criminal records form a substantial institutional barrier to college enrollment. The Chronicle of Higher Education (Lipka 2010) reported that more than 60 percent of U.S. colleges consider applicants' criminal histories when making admissions decisions, and new federal regulations prohibit some individuals with criminal backgrounds from access to financial aid. Direct entry into the workforce is often impeded as well, as demonstrated by Tanner, Davies & O'Grady (1999) who found a significant link between juvenile contact with the criminal justice system and adult unemployment. Perhaps the most damning consequence of juvenile arrest, however, is that individuals who are arrested as juveniles are significantly more likely to be incarcerated as adults than their non-arrested peers (Robins, 1978). With these outcomes viewed coterminously, we can infer that the experience of juvenile arrest goes a long way in precluding social mobility and reinforcing disadvantage on an already vulnerable population.

Building off of this existing body of research, my project seeks to understand whether and when an adolescent is most at risk for experiencing juvenile arrest for the first time and what predicts that risk. Thus, my project will address the following specific research questions: When is an adolescent at risk of being arrested for the first time? Are these risks greater for adolescents who were abused or neglected as children? Do these risks of juvenile arrest associated with childhood abuse or neglect differ by an adolescent's race?

Dataset

This study uses data about adolescent's histories of arrest and abuse originally collected by Widom (1989) and made publically available by the National Institute of Justice (2013). Widom and her colleagues used a specialized cohort design in which abused and neglected children were matched with non-abused and non-neglected children and then followed prospectively into adulthood. Because of the matching procedure, the cohorts are assumed to differ only by the primary risk factor (i.e. having experience childhood maltreatment in the form of substantiated cases of abuse and/or neglect). At the time of collection, none of the subjects had experienced the event of interest (i.e. juvenile arrest). To avoid ambiguity in the temporal ordering of childhood abuse and juvenile arrest, cases were restricted to children who were 11 years old or younger at the time of the abusive incident(s)[1]. Moreover, cohorts were matched and do not differ significantly on the basis of sex, age, race, and approximate socio-economic status. Matching for social class was particularly important because it is theoretically plausible that any relationship between child abuse or neglect and later outcomes is confounded or explained by socio-economic status since substantiated instances of abuse are overrepresented within lower socio-economic groups (MacMillian et al.,2001).This design is particularly appropriate to yield findings with clear implications for developing primary prevention strategies and to suggest interventions to reduce long-term negative consequences of childhood maltreatment.

Measures

Independent Variables

Abuse and Neglect. Cases of abuse or neglect were identified from local juvenile court and probation records in a Midwest metropolitan area. The rationale for identifying the abuse and neglect cases was that these instances were serious enough to come to the attention of either police authorities or child protective services and then brought before a court and adjudicated. Thus, only instances of abuse and neglect that were validated and substantiated by the court are included. "Abuse" refers to cases in which an individual knowingly and willfully inflicted unnecessarily severe corporal punishment or unnecessary physical suffering upon a child, including both physical and sexual abuse. "Neglect" refers to cases in which the court found a child to have no proper parent care or guardianship or to be destitute, homeless, or living in a physically dangerous environment. Neglect cases represent extreme failure to provide adequate food, shelter, and medical attention to children. Excluded were juvenile court cases that represented abused or neglected children that were later adopted, where neglect was deemed "involuntary", or where neglect was constituted only by failure to pay child support. To create the abuse variable, all individuals who did not have a substantiated history of abuse or neglect were coded 0 and all individuals who did have a substantiated history of abuse or neglect were coded 1. Table 1 reports the descriptive statistics for the abused and non-abused cohorts, where 57% of the entire sample experienced abuse and/or neglect and 43% did not. As is clear from the table, the racial composition of the two cohorts is roughly equivalent.

Table 1: Descriptive Statistics of Predictor Variable Abuse (n=1,553)

Race	Abused (N)	Not Abused (N)
Black	32% (282)	35% (232)
White	68% (605)	65% (434)
Total	**57% (887)**	**43% (666)**

Race. The designation of race refers to participants' self-selecting the racial group to which they belong. For the sake of simplicity in statistical modeling, I will focus on only two racial groups: whites and blacks. This decision is also substantively motivated, as the greatest racial disparities in the U.S. criminal justice system have historically been and continue to be between whites and blacks (Alexander, 2010). In the total sample, 33% were black (n=514) and 67% were white (n=1,039). As outlined in Table 1 above, this racial distribution is roughly the same within both the abused and non-abused cohorts as well. To create the race variable, all individuals who identified as white were coded 0 and all who identified as black were coded 1.

Dependent Variable

Juvenile Arrest. The outcome of interest, juvenile arrest, is gathered from official juvenile and criminal court files in the same Midwest metropolitan area. Juvenile arrests refer to any arrest that occurred between age 8 and age 18 and were processed through the juvenile court system. Specifically, "any arrests" refers to both delinquency and status offenses, as well as arrests for any other non-traffic offense. Delinquency implies conduct that does not conform to the legal or moral standards of society and applies only to acts that, if performed by an adult, would be termed criminal. It is thus distinguished from a status offense, a term applied in the United States and other national legal systems to acts considered wrongful when committed by a juvenile but not when committed by an adult. While legally distinguishable, both types of offenses are included under the rubric of juvenile arrest in this sample. It should also be noted that in the dataset, juvenile arrests refers to the first time an individual is arrested as a juvenile. Using survival analysis, once an individual is observed as having been arrested for the first time, he/she is censored from the dataset, thereby precluding biased probability estimates based on individuals that may have been arrested more than once during the period from age 8 to age 18. Like the other dichotomous variables, in order to create the arrest variable, within each discrete time period those who experienced juvenile arrest were coded 1 and those who were not arrested were coded 0. Table 2 displays the descriptive statistics related to the dependent variable arrest, where 22% of all adolescents were arrested for the first time as juvenile.

Table 2: Descriptive Statistics of Dependent Variable Arrest (n=1,553)

Race	Arrested N	Not Arrested N
Black	44% (150)	30% (364)
White	56% (192)	70% (847)
Abused	68% (232)	54% (655)
Not Abused	32% (110)	46% (556)
Total	**22% (342)**	**78% (1,211)**

Quantitative Analysis Procedures

I conducted a discrete-time survival analysis of these data to determine whether and when adolescents were most at risk for juvenile arrest and what predicted that risk. Departing from previous studies that relied primarily on logistic regression techniques, I employed the statistical strategy of discrete time survival analysis. Though survival analysis' application within the social sciences is relatively recent, methodological scholars (Singer & Willett, 2003) have identified it as the best way to identify particularly risky periods within individual's lives and to identify various groups that may be most at risk. Because the primary substantive interest motivating this project is the effect of violent and unstable environments on a child's risk of being swept up into America's overzealous, punitive regime of juvenile justice, my primary predictor of interest was whether or not an adolescent experienced abuse or neglect as a child. Specifically, I investigate whether the risk of juvenile arrest was related to whether an adolescent has experienced abuse or neglect as a child. The secondary substantive motivation is the alarming racial disparity in the juvenile justice system, with black adolescents being disproportionately represented within the incarcerated juvenile population. As such, my second predictor of interest was the adolescent's race, and its relation to the juvenile arrest outcome as well as its interaction with the primary predictor of childhood abuse or neglect. I built a taxonomy of nested logistic hazard models to answer these questions, initially examining the effects of abuse on the risk of juvenile arrest and then examining those risks in the context of race, as well as the interaction between the two. I retained only those predictors and interaction terms significantly related to the risk for juvenile arrest in my final model. Discrete-time models were fit to the data using logistic regression procedures in STATA (Version 13, StataCorp, 2013).

Results

In Table 3, I present the results of fitting a taxonomy of discrete-time survival analysis to age at first juvenile arrest, which includes change-in-deviance statistics hypothesis tests that determine whether adding each of my three predictors (i.e. abuse, race, and the interaction between the two) improved the fit of the previous model. As seen in Table 3, by examining the deviance based hypothesis test results, each predictor makes a significant contribution to the previous model. For example, in Model 2, I concluded that adolescents who were abused and/or neglected prior to age 11 were at a greater risk of being arrested for the first time compared to adolescents who were not abused ($\beta_{abused} = 0.537$, 95% CI [.307, .768], $z = 4.57$, $p < 0.001$). On average, the fitted odds that an adolescent who was abused would be arrested for the first time as a juvenile are 1.71 times the fitted odds for an adolescent who was not abused, holding age constant.

I have determined that Model 4 is the best-fitting model because it has the lowest deviance statistic (-2 LogLikelihood = 3,049.392) and because each of the predictors (which were added one at a time) is a statistically significant predictor of the risk of juvenile arrest (see the four deviance based hypothesis tests). In addition, the Wald hypothesis test for each parameter in the three models indicates that, in each model, the parameter for the added predictor is significant when controlling for the other predictors in the model. Moreover, Model 4 addresses all the substantive research questions outlined at the beginning. Given both the statistical and substantive motivation, I will answer my research questions specifically by interpreting the fitted results of Model 4.

Table 3. Results of Fitting a Taxonomy of Discrete-Time Hazard Models to Age at First Juvenile Arrest (N=1,553, 342 Events)

Variables	Model 1	Model 2	Model 3	Model 4
Age8	-6.653***	-6.994***	-7.239***	-7.102***
	(0.708)	(0.712)	(0.715)	(0.717)
Age 9	-5.038***	-5.378***	-5.623***	-5.485***
	(0.317)	(0.328)	(0.333)	(0.337)
Age 10	-5.137***	-5.477***	-5.720***	-5.582***
	(0.334)	(0.344)	(0.349)	(0.353)
Age 11	-4.229***	-4.567***	-4.809***	-4.671***
	(0.215)	(0.230)	(0.236)	(0.243)
Variables	Model 1	Model 2	Model 3	Model 4
Age 12	-3.969***	-4.306***	-4.546***	-4.407***
	(0.191)	(0.207)	(0.215)	(0.222)
Age 13	-3.814***	-4.148***	-4.384***	-4.245***
	(0.179)	(0.196)	(0.203)	(0.211)

ge 14	-3.374***	-3.708***	-3.941***	-3.801***
	(0.147)	(0.167)	(0.176)	(0.185)
ge 15	-2.887***	-3.217***	-3.448***	-3.307***
	(0.119)	(0.143)	(0.153)	(0.163)
ge 16	-3.016***	-3.345***	-3.571***	-3.429***
	(0.130)	(0.152)	(0.161)	(0.171)
ge 17	-3.449***	-3.773***	-3.995***	-3.852***
	(0.163)	(0.180)	(0.188)	(0.197)
ge 18	-4.320	-4.645***	-4.867***	-4.725***
	(0.252)	(0.264)	(0.269)	(0.275)
bused		0.537***	0.568***	0.360*
		(0.118)	(0.118)	(0.154)
ace (1=Black)			0.568***	0.246
			(0.111)	(0.197)
bused x Race				0.479*
				(0.239)
oodness of fit				
Deviance	3,100.563	3,078.597	3,053.440	3,049.392
Number of Parameters	11	12	13	14
eviance Based ypothesis Test(*df*)				
$H_0{:}\beta_{abused}=0$	21.966***(1)			
$H_0{:}\beta_{race}=0$			25.157(1)***	
$H_0{:}\beta_{abusedxrace}=0$				4.048*(1)
/ald Hypothesis est(*df*)				
$H_0{:}\beta_{abused}=0$		20.88***(1)	23.21***(1)	5.47*(1)
$H_0{:}\beta_{race}=0$			25.97***(1)	1.55(1)
$H_0{:}\beta_{abusedxrace}=0$				4.01*(1)

tandard errors in
arentheses
p<0.05   ***p<0.001

In Model 4, I concluded that there is statistically significant interaction between experiencing abuse or neglect as a child and an adolescent's race in the prediction of the occurrence of juvenile arrest ($\Delta = 4.048$, $df = 1$, $p < .05$). In Figure 1 below I provide a graphical summary of this model by plotting the fitted hazard probabilities describing the probability of being arrested for the first time as juvenile for four prototypical adolescents: a white adolescent who was abused or neglected as a child, a white adolescent who was not neglected, a black adolescent who was abused or neglected, and a black adolescent who was not abused or neglected.[5]

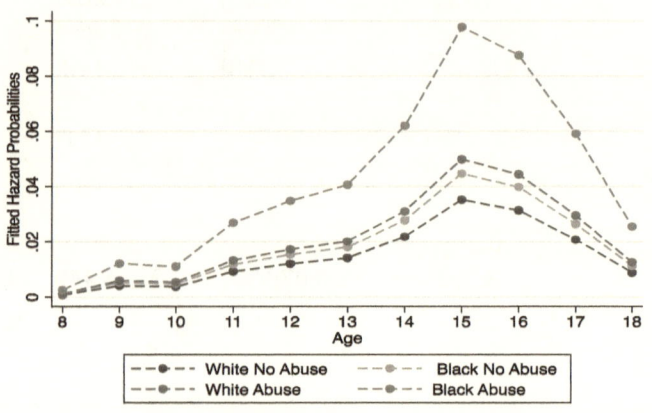

Figure 1. Fitted hazard probabilities describing the probability of being arrested for the first time as juvenile for four prototypical adolescents who either experienced abuse or neglect as a child or not, for both white and black adolescents, respectively. (from Model 4)

We observe that, on average, the fitted risk of an adolescent being arrested as a juvenile is consistently greater at each successive age until age 15 when that risk peaks (remaining quite high at the age of 16), and then begins to decline dramatically (for those who had not been arrested prior to those ages), controlling for race, abuse, and the interaction of race and abuse (as indicated by the identical "peak" of the hazard probability for each prototypical individual).

What stands out most in this fitted plot, however, is the significant interaction between race and abuse ($\beta_{abusedxrace}$ = 0.479, 95% CI [.010,

.947], z = 2.00, p = 0.045). A comparison of hazard functions for whites and blacks reveal that, although being abused leaves children of both races more at risk for being arrested at each age, the effect of abuse on African American children's risk is much greater than that for similarly abused white children. For example, at age 15, when risk of juvenile arrest is highest for all individuals, the fitted hazard probability that a black adolescent who was abused as a child will be arrested is 9.77% (given that the individual had not been arrested before that age). By contrast, at age 15, the fitted hazard probability that a white adolescent who was abused or neglected will be arrested for the first time is 4.99%, a difference of almost 5 percentage points less. Moreover, the risk of juvenile arrest for non-abused youth is 3.53% and 4.47% for whites and blacks, respectively. Another striking comparison is the minuscule risk differential between abused white adolescents and non-abused black adolescents, which at age 15 (when differential is highest) is less than a percentage point (0.52%).

Furthermore, among whites, the odds of first juvenile arrest are 43% higher for adolescents who were abused. Among adolescents who have not been abused or neglected, the odds of first juvenile arrest are 28% higher for blacks in comparison to whites. However, it is black adolescents who have been abused who are at especially great risk of first juvenile arrest. In comparison to their white peers who were not abused, their fitted odds of first arrest are nearly three times as high. This dramatically elevated risk is much greater than the sum of each of the separate risks associated with abuse or race. In other words, it is the co-occurrence of these circumstances—being a black adolescent who has been either abused or neglected as a child—that augurs particularly ill for potential life outcomes.

Similar findings are presented in the fitted survival plots in Figure 2 below, but from the perspective of how long various subgroups of youth "survive" adolescence without being arrested.

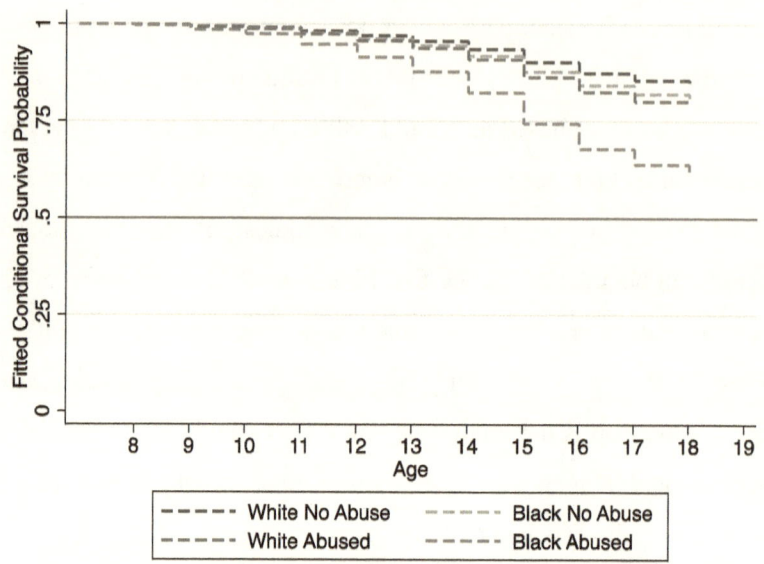

Figure 2. Fitted survival probabilities describing the cumulative probability that an adolescent will survive beyond each discrete age (8-18), without being arrested for the first time, for four prototypical adolescents who either experienced abuse as a child or not, for both black and white adolescents, respectively. (from Model 4).

As the downward trend of the fitted survival probabilities indicate, an increasing number of adolescents are arrested over time (i.e. the function declines as fewer individuals avoid arrest over time). Again we observe a striking difference in probabilities based on the interaction of abuse and race. For African American youth who were abused or neglected, 38% had been arrested for a juvenile crime by age 18. By comparison, of their white counterparts who also experienced abuse or neglect, 21% had been arrested for a juvenile crime by age 18. Thus, amongst adolescents who were abused or neglected, the probability that a white adolescent will survive through adolescence without being arrested for a juvenile crime is about 17 percentage points greater than for a black adolescent. Again, white adolescents who were not abused or neglected survived the longest, with 15% having been arrested for a juvenile crime by the age of 18. Non-abused black adolescents survived at a similar rate, with 19% being arrested for a juvenile crime by age 18.

Overall, the results of my analysis illustrate that the risk of first juvenile arrest is low during childhood, accelerates during the teen years, peaking between ages 15 and 17. I have also found that adolescents who have been abused are consistently at a greater risk for first juvenile arrest than their peers who have not been abused. Moreover, I have found that the effect of abuse differs across racial groups. Among white youth, the risk associated with abuse is certainly notable, but among black youth, it is profound. These findings will be discussed in the next section within the context of racial and theological theories that frame the current discourse around America's draconian regime of justice and punishment.

Discussion

Childhood victimization has demonstrable long-term negative consequences—in particular for child's probability of becoming involved with the juvenile justice system. Though the path from childhood abuse or neglect to juvenile crime is far from inevitable—thankfully not every child who experiences this type of maltreatment is fatalistically doomed for juvenile detention—there is strong evidence to suggest that childhood abuses and juvenile crime are mutually reinforcing phenomena. Yet, this conclusion, distressing and revealing as it is, raises as many questions as it answers. Having observed the close association between child abuse or neglect, race, and juvenile arrest, how are we to make sense of these negative trends and their glaring racial disparity?

Cumulatively, these results indicate that there may be additional factors at play beyond individual circumstances or characteristics. Specifically, egregious racial disparities in the outcome exist such that, even amongst children who have been abused—those identified as most at risk for juvenile arrest—the odds that an African American adolescent will be arrested are 53 % higher in comparison to white abused peers. On its surface, this stark discrepancy may be puzzling. Why, given the similar negative circumstances of abuse, in which blacks and whites were proportionately represented, would these black adolescents be any more likely to be arrested for juvenile crimes than their white counterparts? Especially since other research has shown that youth of all races commit delinquent offenses at roughly equivalent rates (Kirk & Sampson, 2013). When viewed through the lens of America's structural racism, however, the initial confusion over this disparity is mitigated. As Michelle Alexander (2010) explains, racism is not only manifested in individual racial animus, but in the basic structural dimensions of society. Structural racism does not require racist motives, but racist practices. That is, the ways in which individual and institutional behavior interact across domains and over time to produce unintended consequences with clear racialized effects—such as the racial disparities revealed in this analysis of child abuse and juvenile arrest data. These processes are increasingly covert, often racially neutral on their face, but nevertheless succeed in maintaining a racialized status quo that elevates whites and disadvantages people of color. For example, Alexander (2010) cites the racialized practices of the enforcement of America's drug laws, such as discretionary community policing that concentrates in "high crime" ghettos and results in African Americans and Latinos being disproportionately admitted to prison on drug charges, even as rates and patterns of drug use actually indicate that whites are slightly more likely to use or sell illegal drugs. These practices, while neutral on their face, are racialized in practice because these same ghettos disproportionately house people of color, since the ghetto itself was constructed to contain and control groups of people defined by race. Communities of color are therefore systematically targeted for police surveillance, while white communities go tacitly ignored.

My findings corroborate Alexander's ideas of the disproportionate impact of structurally racist practices, as my analysis does more than tell the unfortunate story of what happens to adolescents who have been abused. Instead, what has emerged most strikingly is what happens to black children who have been abused. In looking for clues as to why this might be, there is a large and convincing body of research that documents the significant racial discipline gap amongst adolescents, specifically within schools. For example, 74-94% of schools in the U.S. have zero tolerance discipline policies which impose automatic and exceedingly harsh penalties, including suspension and expulsion, for student offenses (Kirk & Sampson, 2013). These policies have lead to the increasing criminalization of adolescent behavior and a disproportionate number of minority students being suspended, dropping out, or incarcerated (Hatt, 2011; Reyes, 2006). While ostensibly designed to increase safety, these punitive policies mostly serve to treat youth as objects in need of intervention, further disadvantaging already marginalized youth. Moreover, unconscious racial bias, such as views of children of color as community threats, potential gang members or drug dealers rather than youth or students, as well as the fears produced by these beliefs, may lead to increased referrals to juvenile correctional systems (Widom et. al., 2012, Edelman, 2008). Or it is possible that black children who experience abuse or neglect do not have equal access to the proper social services, ending up in the juvenile justice system in lieu of receiving other social support (Rawal, Romansky, Jenuwine, & Lyons, 2004). Whatever the reason, the effect is clear—African American children are disproportionately funneled into the juvenile justice system. And, as Alexander (2010) as well as other theorists (Sampson & Laub, 1997) note, within our justice system what matters even more than the charges is the "criminal" label—even if those black youth arrested are not officially incarcerated in juvenile detention centers, they are being swept up into a punitive system of control that labels them as a "other" and ushers them into a place of perpetual disadvantage within America's racial hierarchy.

This notion of who is "other" is particularly salient for trying to understand my findings about the relationship between child maltreatment, race, and juvenile arrest within the cycles of violence, punishment, and inhumanity undergirding America' present juvenile justice system. Sampson and Laub's (1997) life-course theory suggests that once an individual is labeled deviant (e.g. through an arrest record), a variety of detachment processes are set in motion that promote further deviance and decrease the likelihood of successful transition to adulthood. The theory specifically suggests a "snowball" effect—that adolescent delinquency and its negative consequences (e.g., arrest, official labeling, incarceration) increasingly mortgage one's future, especially later life chances like educational attainment and employment. For example, some labeling theorists have argued that official labels, if accepted by sanctioned youth and their primary groups, inhibit positive identification with the student role and hence with pro-social peers and school authorities (Bernburg & Krohn 2003). Similarly, Moffitt (1993) described how some delinquents become "ensnared" by the consequences of their antisocial behavior, thereby narrowing the opportunities available to them to follow a prosocial behavioral repertoire. The snare of arrest may be an irrevocable event that drastically curtails a delinquent individual's opportunity to "go straight."

As Richard Snyder (2000) argues, once we have a category into which to fit people—problem child, juvenile delinquent, criminal—they can be objectified. According to Snyder, undergirded by Protestant individualized notions of sin and redemption these classifications are often turned into ontological categories that divide people based on assumed essential differences, enabling some persons to be thought of as inferior, thereby reinforcing existing social inequalities and larger structures of alienation and discrimination. This objectification most often happens with those at the margins. As corroborated by my analysis, it was the adolescents who were abused or neglected—and in particular blacks who were abused or neglected—that were consistently at a greater risk for being abandoned to this tragedy of objectification. Being arrested and most often labeled as "problems" those who have already experienced abuse or neglect are put at an even greater disadvantage in overcoming the negative effects of childhood maltreatment, and thus the vicious cycle rages on—arrested students with arrested futures.

With respect to juvenile arrest, the forces at work are multi-layered and complex, reminding us that crime is neither committed, prevented, or prosecuted in a vacuum. As Richard Snyder (2000) argues, all individual decisions are intermingled with social, cultural, physical, and psychological forces that influence individuals towards certain paths of action. As we can infer from this analysis, an adolescent's involvement in a crime often contains layers of forces which influence that decision, including (but certainly not limited to) the forces of abuse and neglect that wield their power to constrain the life choices of those affected. When we lose sight of the umbilical connection between criminal acts and the larger social collectivity, we risk dealing with crime by dealing with those who commit crimes as isolates. But this reductive individualism belies our complex social reality. The fact is, when children who have been abused or neglected are at risk for getting swept up into cycles of violence and instability, the onus falls on us all. According to Snyder, it is Protestant Christianity's individualized notions of sin and grace, which place all responsibility for transgressions and redemption on the individual, conveniently denying the larger community's complicity—its choices, polices, structures—that bifurcates the world into the redeemed and unredeemed, the worth and unworthy, criminals and victims. Eschewing collective responsibility and assigning blame too narrowly on those who commit criminal offenses only exacerbates the retributive nature of our justice system and fuels the spirit of punishment that leads America to arrest more than 4,000 children every day and incarcerate more than 2 million adults and some 70,000 children.

Echoing Snyder's assessment of America's toxic individualism, Lawrence Friedman (1993) notes that the American system of criminal justice has always professed deep concern for the self, making claims that every person accused of a crime is a unique individual, tailoring guilt, innocence and just deserts to the order of the individual. But as Friedman, and the analysis above remind us, crime is the statistical companion of social disorganization. No theory of crime, he argues, can ignore the social backgrounds of those who commit crimes. For even as American society exalts the individual, human beings are inherently social. As such, we cannot and should not naïvely read the results of the analysis above as demonstrative of the moral failings of those arrested adolescents. Rather, heeding Snyder's call to collective responsibility, these results are best understood within the context of social accountability to all children who are at risk for getting caught in vicious cycles of violence and social instability. What can we, as a society, do to reduce the likelihood that any child will be abused or arrested in the first place? For those who have been abused, how can we assure they receive proper care and reduce the likelihood that they will resort to violence themselves? But perhaps the most troubling question to ask ourselves is the extent to which we, both as individuals and as a society, have been complicit in the creation and sustaining of a system which produces such devastating outcomes for so many of our children? These questions raised by the data are perhaps the most important of my results. To begin to address them, we must not look solely at the individuals directly involved, but must turn the spotlight back around on ourselves and ask: What does accountability mean?

Behind every fact is a face. Behind every statistic is a story. Behind every academic buzzword is a young person whose future will be lost if something is not done immediately to change his or her reality. The numbers are staggering and the reality is sobering. In advocating for an alternative to our current crisis of mass punishment, Snyder invokes the South African philosophy of Ubuntu—I am because we are. This philosophy emphasizes the goodness, dignity, and integrity of all persons and affirms our mutual dependency. Archbishop Desmond Tutu describes, "A person is human precisely in being enveloped in the community of other human beings, in being caught up in the bundle of life. To be is to participate"(Snyder, 2001, pg. 106). To counter the vicious cycle of violence, retribution, and objectification that characterizes our current juvenile justice system, I argue that this philosophy of mutual respect and interdependence be embraced and enacted for all our children. Our collective future turns, to a great extent, on what the young do and what is done to them. We owe it to ourselves, and our children, to allow everyone the fullest rights of participation—to shed the vicious cycle in order to be enveloped by a virtuous, life-affirming one. Accountability need not mandate retributive punishment, but accountability to one another's humanity as our own.

Endnotes

1. This age restriction helped to more clearly indicate the temporal sequence between exposure to abuse/neglect and the outcome of juvenile arrest. Specifically, in cases in which delinquency may have preceded abuse and/or neglect or may have been the cause of the abuse or neglect should not be included. Thus, to ensure that the order of temporal sequence was clear (abuse/neglect ➞ arrest), abuse and neglect cases are restricted by age.

2. For reasons related to confidentiality, the specific city is not named.

3. Given that only substantiated cases of abuse or neglect are included, one possible limitation is that the results reported here might be underestimations of the effects of abuse or neglect, since many instances of child maltreatment go unreported.

4. "Involuntary" neglect are cases in which the mother or other legal guardian is temporarily unavailable to provide for a child because of institutionalization in a mental health facility, medical hospital, prison, or jail.

5. Interaction effects are interpreted by simultaneously considering all constituent parameters for the interaction term and its main effect components. In this case, we consider simultaneously the effects of β_{abused}, β_{race}, $\beta_{abusedxrace}$. As all these predictors are dichotomies, this leads to the consideration of four prototypical individuals who represent all possible combination of abused and race.

Bibliography

Alexander, M., (2010). *The new jim crow: Mass incarceration in the age of colorblindness.* New York, NY: The New Press.

Bernburg, J.G. and Krohn, M.D. (2003). "Labeling, Life Chances, and Adult Crime: The Direct and Indirect Effects of Official Intervention in Adolescence on Crime in Early Adulthood." Criminology 41(4):1287-1318.

Bernburg, J.G, Krohn, M.D. and Rivera, C.J. (2006). "Official Labeling, Criminal Embeddedness, and Subsequent Delinquency: A Longitudinal Test of Labeling Theory." Journal of Research in Crime and Delinquency 43(1):67-88

Children's Defense Fund, *The State of America's Children 2014.* Washington D.C.: Children's Defense Fund. http://www.childrensdefense.org/child-research-data-publications/state-of-americas-children/ (Accessed April 14, 2014).

Data Resources Program. (2013). *National Institute of Justice.* Retrieved from http://www.nij.gov/funding/data-resources-program/Pages/welcome.aspx (accessed April 4, 2014)

Edelman, M.W. (2008). *The sea is so wide and my boat is so small.* New York, NY: Hyperion.

Ferguson, D.M., & Lynskey, M.T. (1997). Physical punishment/maltreatment during childhood and adjustment in young adulthood. *Child Abuse and Neglect*, 21, 617-630.

Forman, J., (2012) "Racial critiques of mass incarceration: Beyond the new jim crow." *New York University Law Review,* 87, 21-69.

Freidman, L.M., (1993). *Crime and punishment in American history.* New York, NY: BasicBooks.

Garland, D. (2001). *Mass imprisonment social causes and consequences.* London: SAGE

Hatt, B. (2011). "Still I rise: Youth caught between the worlds of schools and prisons." *Urban Review*, 43, 476-490.

Ireland, T.O., Smith, C.A. & Thornberry, T.P. (2002). Developmental issues in the impact of child maltreatment on later delinquency and drug use. *Criminology, 40*, 359-399.

Kirk, D. & Sampson, R.J. (2013). "Juvenile arrest and collateral educational damage in the transition to adulthood." *Sociology of Education*, 86, 36-62.

Lansford, J.E., Dodge, K.A., Petit, G.S., Bates, J.E., Crozier, J., & Kaplow J. (2002). A 12-year prospective study of the long-term effects of early child physical maltreatment on psychological, behavioral, and academic problems in adolescence. *Archives of Pediatrics and Adolescent Medicine*, 156, 824-830.

Lipka, S. (2010). "Experts Debate Fairness of Criminal-Background Checks on Students." Chronicle of Higher Education. Retrieved from: (http://chronicle.com/article/Experts-Debate   -Fairness-of/66107/?sid=at). (accessed May 2, 2014).

MacMillan, H.L., Fleming, J.E., Streiner, D.L., Lin, E., Boyle, M., Jamieson, E., Duku, E.K., Walsh, C.A., Wong, M.Y.Y., Beardslee, W.R. (2001) "Childhood abuse and lifetime psychopathology in a community sample." *American Journal of Psychiatry*, 158, 1878-1883.

Mendel, Richard A. *No Place for Kids: The Case for Reducing Juvenile Incarceration*. The Annie E. Casey Foundation. Retrieved from http://www.aecf.org/~/media/Pubs/Topics/Juvenile%20Justic e/Detention%20Reform/NoPlaceForKids/JJ_NoPlaceForKids_F ull.pdf (accessed April 20, 2014).

Moffitt, T.E. (1993). "Adolescence-limited and Life-Course-persistent Antisocial Behavior: A Developmental Taxonomy." Psychological Review 100(4):674-701. OJJDP Statistical Briefing Book. "Juveniles on Probation." Office of Juvenile Justice Delinquency Prevention.   Retrieved from:http://www.ojjdp.gove/ojstabb/Probation/qa07102.asp? qaDate=2010(accessed April 15, 2014).

Rawal, P., Romansky, J., Jenuwine, M., Lyons, J.S. (2004). "Racial differences in the mental health needs and service utilization of youth in the juvenile justice system. *Journal of Behavioral Health Services and Research,* 31, 242-254.

Reyes, A. (2006). "The criminalization of student discipline programs and adolescent behavior." *Journal of Civil Rights and Economic Development,* 21, 73-110.

Robins, L.N. (1978). "Sturdy Childhood Predictors of Adult Antisocial Behaviour: Replications from Longitudinal Studies." Psychological Medicine 8(4):611-22.

Rogosch, F.A., Cicchetti, D., & Aber, J.L. (1995). The role of child maltreatment in early deviations in cognitive and affective processing abilities and later peer relationship problems. *Development and Psychopathology,* 7, 591-609.

Sampson, Robert J. and John H. Laub. 1997. "A Life-Course Theory of Cumulative Disadvantage and the Stability of Delinquency." In Developmental Theories of Crimeand Delinquency (Advances in Criminological Theory, Vol. 7), edited by T. P. Thornberry. New Brunswick, NJ: Transaction.

Singer, J.D., & Willett, J.B. (2003) *Applied longitudinal data analysis: Modeling change and event occurrence.* New York: Oxford University Press.

Snyder, T.R., (2000). *The protestant ethic and the spirit of punishment.* Grand Rapids, MI: Wm. B. Eerdmans Publishing Co.

StataCorp. 2013. *Stata Statistical Software: Release 13.* College Station, TX: StataCorp LP.

Stouthamer-Loeber, M., Loeber, R., Homish, D.L., & Wei, E. (2001). Maltreatment of boys and the development of disruptive and delinquent behavior. *Development and Psychopathology,* 13, 941-955.

Tanner, J., Davies, S., a O'Grady, B. (1999). Whatever happened to yesterday's rebels? Longitudinal effects of youth delinquency on education and employment. Social Forces, 46, 250-274.

The Annie E. Casey Foundation (2013). *Reducing youth incarceration in the United States.* Retrieved from http://www.aecf.org/~/media/Pubs/Initiatives/KIDS%20COUNT/R /ReducingYouthIncarcerationSnapshot/DataSnapshotYouthIncarce ration.pdf (accessed May 1, 2014)

The Sentencing Project . "Prison population, 1980 - 2011." The Sentencing Project Interactive Map. Retrieved from: http://www.sentencingproject.org/map/map/.cfm#map (accessed April 14, 2014) .

Widom, C.S. (1989). Child abuse, neglect, and violent criminal behavior. *Criminology*, 27(2), 251-271.

Widom, C.S., Czaja, S., Wilson, H.W., Allwood, M., Chauhan, P., (2012). "Do the long-term consequences of neglect differ for children of different races and ethic backgrounds?". *Child Maltreatment*, 18, 42-55.

Unlocking the Potential

Steven A. Quinlan

Ever since the 1805 opening of the first state prison in Charlestown, prisons have served Massachusetts residents as the primary response to crime in their communities. Today Massachusetts contributes more than 11,000[2] men and women to the estimated 2.3 million people incarcerated nationally.[3] The Massachusetts Department of Corrections (DOC) considers preparing people who are incarcerated for release back to the community, either by parole, probation, or completion of their sentence, one of its primary objectives toward promoting public safety.[4] Since the DOC currently operates as a contingent of 18 facilities with levels of security ranging from pre-release/minimum to super-maximum,[5] the multiple prisons effectively function as a means to prevent people who have sacrificed their right to live in a free society from having access to it. In this, it is deduced that, by "promoting public safety," the DOC means that its primary objective is in preserving "the welfare and protection of the general public" by preventing people who have already exhibited criminal behavior from committing further crime.[6]

A key strategy that the DOC claims to employ in order to accomplish this task is through "partnering with educational organizations" to equip people who are incarcerated with skills that are necessary to succeed in the free world.[7] In fact, studies consistently demonstrate that access to education, particularly post-secondary, i.e. college-level or vocational instruction,[8] contributes to the correctional mission of secure facilities and safe communities by "improving [people's] behavior on the inside and promoting success after release.[9] However, with merely 2.2 percent of the DOC budget allocated to education and rehabilitative programming,[10] the DOC does not appear to recognize educating incarcerated people as a major public safety priority.

As a result, MGT of America, a nationwide firm with specialists in corrections, law enforcement, and public safety, expressed concern with several areas of the Massachusetts DOC Public Safety Strategy, including a sub-adequate curriculum of educational and vocational training.[11] Indeed, post-secondary education is scarcely available to people who are incarcerated. In 1994, Federal Pell Grants that were commonly used to provide post-secondary education to incarcerated students were legislatively eliminated,[12] all but decimating incarcerated people's access to college-level or vocational education.

Presently, no Massachusetts DOC funds are allotted to post secondary education. However, federal funding is available. For example, the Workplace and Community Transition Training for Incarcerated Individuals offers financial assistance to incarcerated people up to the age of 35 and within seven years of release.[13] In addition, the Carl D. Perkins Vocational and Applied Technology Act offers no more than one percent of its funds for correctional vocational programs.[14] Even still, nationwide less than 5 percent of incarcerated people actively participate in post-secondary educational or vocational programs. Undeniably, as MGT of America had reported, more needs to be done.

Consequently, by utilizing in-class texts, particularly Michel Foucault's *Discipline and Punish: The Birth of the Prison* and Lawrence M. Friedman's *Crime and Punishment in American History*, along with other germane primary and supplementary sources, this paper will trace the intended purpose of incarceration, specifically as a form of corporal punishment that has evolved from targeting the body of the accused person to today's "economy of suspended rights," where it is intended that a person's desire for the basic liberties associated with the American concept of freedom, i.e. free movement, free speech, and the right to free participation in the democratic government will serve to correct her criminal behavior.[16]

Further, in his book *In Defense of Flogging*, Peter Moskos addresses what he considers the gross ineffectiveness of incarceration as it stands today, and calls for a return back to corporal punishment, which he argues, paradoxically, is a more "humane" and pragmatic approach to correcting criminal behavior. Similarly, Michelle Alexander calls foul against the current incarceration system and illustrates how punishment for criminal behavior unjustly follows people post-incarceration through social stigma and employer discrimination. The resulting unemployment, emasculation, and personal frustration that this reality elicits, argues Alexander, fosters an atmosphere of economic-related crime.

Regardless of the intended target, the common theme within the literature is, unavoidably, punishment. In essence, punishment is inflicted on the body of the accused or by stripping his cherished liberties, but what has yet to be addressed is the mind of the accused.

Statistics show that people who are incarcerated are "much less educated than their counterparts in mainstream society.[17] In fact, the majority of people incarcerated in Massachusetts State Prisons "function educationally at less than a high school level."[18] Therefore, by examining the effect that cognitive development has on individual decision-making, behavior, employability, and recidivism, it is the intention of this study to answer one specific question: How does providing post-secondary education to people who are incarcerated impact public safety, i.e., reduce crime, in the state of Massachusetts?

In reflecting upon the early examples of fortified prisons, it is difficult not to be reminded of the multitude of slave fortresses that once peppered the West African coastline. Massive structures constructed by indestructible concrete and iron, teemed with malnourished and severely maltreated people; hopeless souls guilty of, and punished for, committing one unavoidable crime: being black! The intended purpose of these prisons, then, was undeniably to "render individuals docile" by their restricted movement, and "useful" by their future enslavement.[19]

The early American concept of prison embodied a similar philosophy, i.e., to punish the body by incapacitating a person from the ability to cause further public harm. As a result, prisons materialized into "a human dumping grounds" where people who were convicted of committing crime were essentially sentenced to "wallow in a putrid mire demoralizing to the body and soul."[20] In essence, early prisons addressed public safety by simply locking people into decrepit dungeons and vigorously working them until their release, or worse, death. Thus, punishment remained a primary factor of incarceration and slavery was its accomplice.[21]

The 20th century, however, witnessed an awakening in public consciousness about the mistreatment of society's marginalized minorities. Civil-Rights demonstrations increased national and international awareness to southern injustice and dark prison secrets were equally exposed. For instance, incarcerated people began filing lawsuits and were successful in illuminating the horrendous "inhuman conditions" within federal, state, and county prisons.[22] Consequently, new rhetoric, such as "Rehabilitation and job-training" were incorporated into the mission of incarcerating people convicted of committing crime.[23]

Today, prisons are still massive fortresses of concrete and steel, merely with modernized architecture and technology. Federal health standards now ensure people living in these facilities are no longer malnourished and their quality of treatment, though better protected by law, remains debatable. While punishment for criminal activity is still a fundamental purpose of the modern prison system, "preparing people for successful reentry," whether by parole, probation, or sentence completion, is an equally stated priority.[24] Nevertheless, facilitating such "preparation" can become complicated.

The Massachusetts Department of Corrections claims that its mission is to "provide care and appropriate programming" to people who are incarcerated in order to promote public safety.[25] Many factors have to be considered in order to realize this goal. For instance, care and appropriate programming must include, among other things, mental health, anger management, and cognitive development. Evidence has consistently pointed to education as the most effective crime deterrent[26] For this reason the

Federal Bureau of Prisons "mandates" participation in education below a certain level.[27] Similarly, in 2014, Massachusetts DOC initiated its "Program Engagement Strategy" in which it intends to encourage people with less than a high school education to participate in high school equivalency programs like GED or Hi-SET.[28]

Research has consistently demonstrated that certain levels of education are a "prerequisite to moral thinking."[29] Stanford Law Professor and acclaimed author Lawrence M. Friedman supports this theory by suggesting that "crime is behavior: and its roots must lie somewhere in the personality, character, and culture of the people who do the acts we condemn."[30] In other words, if criminal behavior is not a result, as some may believe, of an inherent criminal character-trait, such conduct if properly addressed can be corrected. However in a nation where more than 1 in every 100 adults is in prison or jail[31] and with 1 in 31 under some form of correctional control, i.e., parole, probation, or house arrest,[32] it is in the interest of public safety that the citizens of Massachusetts make an informed investment into facilitating this change.

Post-secondary education is the ideal medium for nurturing cognitive development and promoting positive self-worth. The critical-thinking skills that accompany cognitive development have a significant impact on public safety because they improve individual decision-making and equip incarcerated students with applicable pro-social values. In fact, "liberal studies," according to the Journal of Correctional Education, "can alter prisoners' perceptions of others while also promoting moral development that alters the way in which they interpret their perceptions, and ultimately how they behave."[33] In essence, when an incarcerated student is enabled to critically analyze complex philosophical texts like Albert Camus *The Rebel*, or intellectually respond to writings that address important social issues, she becomes empowered to critically examine her own physical and social condition and make decisions that reflect better judgment during and post incarceration.

The confidence that accompanies the ability to think critically dramatically increases an incarcerated student's self-esteem. Instilling positive self-worth in people who are incarcerated is instrumental in promoting public safety because it affords them an opportunity to explore and better understand their own potential.[34] Lack of education is directly associated with low self-regard because it hinders an individual's ability to effectively communicate with others which consequently often manifests through "limited respect for others and institutions.[35]

In fact, low self-esteem is a notorious precursor to gang affiliation. When a person lacks self-confidence, he becomes consumed by a desire to be accepted by his peers. Since loyalty and mischievous group-activity are celebrated gang values, gangs immediately satisfy a desperate person's "appeal of being an integral part of a group.[36]

Urban communities throughout the state of Massachusetts suffer extremely high rates of gang activity. Moreover, these street gangs are directly influenced by and inter-related with prison gangs. Gang culture depends exclusively on individual and collective reputations and various levels of peer-group respect that are specifically predicated on either their will and/or potential to employ violence.[37] However, elevated self-esteem essentially serves as a shield against the enticements of dangerous gangs, thereby fortifying the community by safeguarding the individual.[38]

An additional and certainly equal contribution to public safety that post-secondary education provides is its remarkable influence on post-release employment. Former US Department of Corrections Secretary Margaret Spellings had stated that "90 percent of the fastest growing jobs require post-secondary education or training.[39] Most estimates show that, nationally, nearly 97 percent of the nation's incarcerated population will eventually be released and return home to communities across the country.[40] With just under 5 percent of those returning citizens having access to post-secondary education,[41] 90 percent of those released will be ineligible for 90 percent of the fastest growing jobs. These numbers suggest that tens of thousands of returning citizens will either be unemployed or under-employed, which undoubtedly translates into increased public safety charges and high-rates of economic-based crime.

In 2010, more than 10 percent, or more than half of a million Massachusetts residents were living below the national poverty line.[42] That same year Massachusetts residents became victims of nearly 150,000 crimes that can be directly traced to economic motivation.[43] This is significant because, nationally, the income of those workers with a Bachelor degree was, on average, 93 percent higher than those with only a high school diploma.[44] Meanwhile, the majority of the more than 11,000 people currently incarcerated in Massachusetts prisons function below a high school level.[45]

The Massachusetts DOC makes it clear that its goal is to promote public safety by preparing an inmate for release to the community and decrease the likelihood of criminal activity.[46] But without equipping people with the skills that are necessary to sustain adequate employment, all that the DOC is really preparing people who are incarcerated for is the revolving door.

Employment is an omni-present obstacle for all returning citizens. Ohio State University Law Professor Michelle Alexander points out that "many employers refuse to consider people with criminal records for a wide range of jobs," despite federal bans on the practice.[47] The reality is that after their release from prison, returning citizens experience enormous prejudice and legal discrimination in their pursuit of sustainable employment. Indeed, "discrimination against people with criminal histories is permissible" depending on the nature of the crime;[48] for instance, people convicted of sexually-related crimes are barred from any public employment that involves young children. However, many other employers have extra-legal motivations, thereby denying returning citizens employment out of pure prejudice.

On the other hand, the potential for a post-secondary degree to counter occupational discrimination is worth commenting on. The fact that a person utilized her incarceration toward academic or vocational self-development speaks volumes for her character. Naturally, when she exhibits such remarkable resilience, she may sway an on-the-fence employer to take a chance. "We believe that when we are able to work and earn a higher-education degree while in prison, we are empowered to truly pay our debt to society," pleads a woman who is incarcerated at MCI Framingham.[49] In essence, the education provides her with a credible voice that has the power to persuade potential employers to measure her redemption by her merit instead of by her label.

The most logical indicator of success or failure of the DOC in promoting public safety, admittedly, is how many people return to prison after being released, i.e., the recidivism rate. After all, the vision statement of the Massachusetts DOC is to "effect positive behavioral change in order to eliminate violence, victimization, and recidivism."[50] Each year Massachusetts taxpayers invest over half of a billion dollars to help the DOC realize its vision.[51] This equates to nearly $46,000 per year, or approximately $885 per week, per incarcerated person. In comparison, the median weekly earnings for an employed person holding an Associates degree in 2011 was $719, just below the total average weekly earnings of $797 for all US employees.[52] In this light it seems reasonable for Massachusetts residents to expect a favorable return on their investment.

From 2004 to 2009 the DOC spent nearly $3 billion in an effort to "eliminate" recidivism.[53] However, the DOC failed to even reduce the number of people recidivating. During this five-year period Massachusetts' incarcerated population grew over 17 percent - a full 10 percent higher than the national average.[54] In fact, some studies even predict that by 2019, the DOC can expect a staggering 30.3 percent increase in its population growth. Granted, some of this growth can be attributed to first-time violators, yet a nearly 50 percent state recidivism rate shows that a large contribution to the population increase can be directly attributed to recidivism. Certainly, with regard to its self-professed vision, the DOC must concede defeat.

Massachusetts boasted a 44 percent recidivism rate in 2010, nearly 25 percent lower than the national rate reported.[55] Still, a 68 percent national recidivism rate is astronomical; so, even though Massachusetts' recidivism rate was substantially less than the national average, 44 percent is nothing worth bragging about. Furthermore, in 2010 nearly 65 percent of all people who reentered Massachusetts communities, whether through parole, probation, or a completed sentence, were directly released from either medium or maximum security, which combined suffered a recidivism rate greater than 52 percent.[56] Therefore, if the measure of success in promoting public safety depends on eliminating, or even reducing, recidivism, Massachusetts residents should seriously reevaluate their investment.

If reducing recidivism is truly a major priority of the Massachusetts citizenry, there are virtually two options at their disposal to make it a reality. One option would be to demand the state legislature to take a dramatically lenient turn in criminal legislation, which would reduce the number of acts considered to be criminal, thereby reducing crime by literally reducing crime. Certainly, while changing legislation may be a no-brainer in some cases, especially with laws in which longer sentences were implemented in an effort to deter similar acts, evidence shows that the threat of punishment, in fact, does not significantly diminish criminal motive. Peter Moskos points out that "deterrence and punishment are separate issues. Punishment is about retribution," but in addressing recidivism, harsher punishment is merely a prescription to a symptom of criminal thinking, i.e., the action, as opposed to the more important disease; that is, what motivates such behavior, or, simply put, lack of education.[57]

The remaining, and most effective fact-supported solution to Massachusetts' colossal recidivism rate is through introducing a vigorous educational curriculum. In 2004, a 25-50 percent decrease in recidivism was noted for prisoners who had attended education programs.[58] Since most incarcerated people function at less than a high school level, secondary education is a fundamental necessity; indeed, "the more literate the individual, the more that he or she may benefit from all other forms of training."[59] But the buck can not stop with a high school equivalent, reducing recidivism urgently depends on more.

For instance, while all education favorably impacts recidivism, nothing can compare with post-secondary education as the, hands down, ultimate promoter of public safety. In 2008, for individuals with a four-year degree, the national recidivism rate plummeted to a staggering 1 to 11 percent![60] Moreover, for the few who had recidivated, overall they committed "less serious offenses compared to their original offense for which they had been in prison."[61] The reality is that even those who are educated may still have other underlying issues that need to be addressed, like drug dependence or anger management for example.[62] Nonetheless, a three state recidivism study between Maryland, Minnesota, and Ohio revealed that the overwhelming majority of people who returned to society with a post-secondary education "no longer commit crime and choose to work in lawful jobs, pay taxes, and support their families."[63]

Essentially, the more education an incarcerated person receives, the less likely she will be re-arrested or re-incarcerated. Unfortunately, though, the current recidivism rate is so high because of the disheartening lack of resources available to address the educational needs of most incarcerated people.

As of January 2010, the prisons in the Massachusetts DOC were a combined 140 percent over-occupied.[64] The DOC recognizes that "overcrowding can have an adverse effect on inmates and staff and can have a profound effect on public safety."[65] This is because people who are incarcerated are being discriminately denied educational and vocational resources based on their sentence structures and criminal histories. Naturally, many people internalize this discrimination as a sign that they are not worthy of being invested in, which has a predictable effect on their self-image and behavior.

Consequently, the majority of these men and women will be released into the community "unskilled, under-educated, and highly likely to become re-involved with criminal activity."[66] US Department of Education Adult Education Director John Linton claims that "we educate inmates in prison so that they will be something other than inmates during subsequent phases of their lives."[67] Indeed, education is an invaluable utility for individual and, consequently, social transformation.

It goes without saying, then, that without adequate care and appropriate programming, returning citizens are essentially "ill prepared to acclimate to the rigors of rejoining society as productive citizens who will not endanger public safety."[68] Again, the DOC chooses to set aside a mere 2.2 percent of its budget to finance such a momentous goal of eliminating recidivism in order to promote public safety. It should then come as no surprise that a pitiful 1.8 percent of full-time DOC staff are in the education department.[69]

With such an insignificant investment, it seems that the decision-makers at the DOC have yet to heed to Mr. Linton's message, and the Massachusetts public continues to pay the price in reduced public safety. Meanwhile, what the DOC does quite successfully accomplish with its half of a billion annual dollars is to "warehouse" incarcerated people until they become someone else's concern.[70]

To be fair, the DOC does provide some post-secondary education services. The Boston University Prison Education Program has existed for more than forty years, collaborating with the DOC to offer an opportunity for approximately 150 people who are incarcerated within three state institutions: MCI Norfolk, MCI Framingham, and Bay State Correctional Center, to acquire an Inter-Disciplinary Bachelors degree. Moreover, the

Prison Education Program was able to persevere through the 1994 Pell Grant fiasco thanks, not to an overwhelming public support for the program, but to the fact that it self-sustains through private funding raised exclusively by Boston University personnel.

Likewise, the Massachusetts DOC also offers limited vocational training at various prisons statewide. Indeed, vocational education can not be overlooked as an important contributor to public safety. In 2010, statistics show a 12.6% reduction in recidivism for people released with a vocational skill.[71] While this reduction is not as pronounced as that of an academic post-secondary education, it can not be denied that for every one crime avoided the streets of Massachusetts become significantly safer. Collectively, all educational opportunities have a dramatic impact on public safety; so whether it is through academic or vocation training, it will be in the best interest of public safety for Massachusetts residents to invest in the post-secondary education of its disadvantaged incarcerated population.

In conclusion, providing post-secondary education to people who are incarcerated has an enormous positive impact on public safety in the state of Massachusetts. The self-confidence and social awareness that post-secondary education nurtures enhances people's decision-making skills and improves their behavior. In addition, post-secondary education also helps returning citizens become more sustainably employed post-release, which undeniably diminishes the motive for economic-based crime, i.e., reducing recidivism. The impact of preventing a single crime from taking place in the streets is immeasurable: a mother not mugged, a sister not raped, a son not murdered. The Massachusetts DOC recognizes the transformative potential that post-secondary education has on personal development and public safety, that's why it supports post-secondary education within its various institutions. However, as MGT of America reported, with 2.2 percent of its budget invested in educational resources, there is still much more to be done.

End Notes

1. Friedman, James. Crime and Punishment in American History.
    New York: Basic Books, 1993; at 74.
2. Massachusetts Department of Corrections "Strategic Plan 2010-
    2015. II at 13.
3. "From the Classroom to the Community: Exploring the Role of
    Education during incarceration and Reentry." Brazzell,
    Crayton, Mukamal, Solomon, Lindhal. The Urban Institute.
    2009, at 1.
4. DOC "Strategic Plan 2010-2015". Supra, at 4, 23.
5. DOC " Strategic Plan 2010-2015 " Supra , at 4.
6. Black's Law Dictionary, 9th ed. Thomson-Rueters, 2009.
7. DOC "Strategic Plan 2010-2015." Supra, at 23.
8. Urban Institute. Supra, at 10.
9. Urban Institute. Supra, at 17.
10. Massachusetts Department of Corrections 2010 annual report, at 44.
11. DOC "Strategic Plan 2010-2015." Supra, at 14.
12. Institute for Higher Education policy (IHEP) "Learning to Reduce
    recidivism: A SO-State Analysis of Post-Secondary Correctional
    Education policy." Erisman and Contardo. November, 2005, at 28.
13. Urban Institute. Supra, at 15.
14. IHEP. Supra, at 28.
15. IHEP. Supra, at 16.
16. Foucault, Michel. Discipline and Punish: The Birth of the
    Prison. New York: Second Vintage, 1995; at 11.
17. IHEP. Supra, at 3.
18. DOC "Strategic Plan 2010-2015." Supra, at 19.
19. Foucault. Supra, at 231.
20. Friedman. Supra, at 310.
21. Moskos, Peter. In Defense of Flogging. New York: Basic Books, 2011;
    at 21.
22. Friedman. Supra, at 309
23. Moskos. Supra, at 6.
24. Massachusetts Department of Corrections 2010 Annual Report, at 5.
25. DOC 2010 Annual report. Supra, at 5.

26. Research Brief, "Education as Crime Prevention: Providing Education to
    Prisoners." Center on Crimes, Communities, and Culture. September,
    1997; at 6.
27. Urban Institute. Supra, at 12.
28. DOC 2010 Annual Report. Supra, at 15.

29. Gaes, Gerald G. "The Impact of Prison education on Post Release Outcomes." February 18, 2008.
30. Friedman. Supra, at 11.
31. Urban institute. Supra, at 1.
32. IHEP. Supra, at 4.
33. Rose, Jane E. and Marilyn Voss. "The Unity in Community: Fostering Academic success Among Diverse communities of Male Offenders in Correctional institutions." The Journal of Correctional education, December, 2003; at 151.
34. Urban institute. Supra, at 17.
35. Rose-Voss. supra, at 137.
36. Lauer, Robert H. and Jeanette Lauer. Social Problems and the Quality of Life. New York: McGraw-Hill, 2006; at 108.
37. Cahill, Spencer E. and Kent Sandstrom. Inside Social Life. 6th ed. New York: Oxford University Press, 2011; at 178-179.
38. Rose-Voss. Supra, at 138.
39. Urban Institute. supra, at 8.
40. Steurer. Infra, at 10.
41. IHEP. Supra, at 3.
42. 2012 World Almanac, at 53.
43. 2012 World Almanac, at 121.
44. Source: Bureau of labor Statistics: Current Population survey 2011.
45. DOC "Strategic Plan 2010-2015." Supra, at 19
46. DOC "Strategic Plan 2010-2015." Supra, at 23.
47. Alexander, Michelle. The New Jim Crow: Mass-Incarceration in the Age of Colorblindness. New York: New Press, 2012; at 153.
48. Alexander. Supra, at 154.
49. Partakers: College Behind Bars: Web Page. Http://www.partakers.org/ sponsor.html. 4-23-08.
50. DOC Annual Report. Supra, at 5.
51. Massachusetts Prison Population Trends 2009. June 2010. Linda Griffin, Hollie Mathews, Susan McDonald, et al.; at 12.

52. Bureau of Labor Statistics. Supra.
53. Population Trends. Supra, at 12.
54. Massachusetts Department of Corrections Ten-Year Prison population Projections. 2009-2019; at 8,12,13.
55. Massachusetts Prison Population Trends 2010. Linda Griffn, Hollie Matthews, Susan McDonald et al. August, 2011; at 45.
56. DOC Annual Reports. supra, at 42.
57. Moskos. Supra, at 23.

58. DOC Stats: The MA Department of Corrections (DOC) by the Number. Angela Antoniewicz. August 2004.
59. Gaes. Supra, at 12.
60. Partakers. Supra.
61. Steurer, Stephen J., and Linda G. Smith. "Education Reduces Crime: Three-State recidivism Study, Feb 2003; at 12.
62. Gaes. Supra, at 12.
63. Steurer. Supra, at 2.
64. DOC "Strategic Plan 2010-2015."_Supra, at 16.
65. DOC "Strat-egic Plan 2010-2015." Supra, at 15.
66. Research Brief. Supra, at 2.
67. Rose-Voss. Supra, at 137.
68. DOC 2010 Annual report. Supra, at 3.
69. DOC 2010 Annual Report. Supra, at 44.
70. Haas Report on the MA Department of Corrections 2011, at 8.
71. Evidence-Based Corrections Programs: What Works & What Does not. Steve Aos, Marna Miller, and Elizabeth Drake. Washington State Institute for public Policy. Jan. 2006, at 3.

Uncaptive Minds and Hearts: Boston University Prison Education Program, Its Impact on Student Rehabilitation

Silvia

"Boston University has given me what I always needed; direction, guidance, and purpose." -current Boston University Prison Education Student, MCI-Norfolk

The above quotation comes from the reflections of a student in the Boston University Prison Education Program at MCI-Norfolk. This student has found a refuge from the dehumanizing environment of correctional institutions and a sense of purpose by participating in this program. His words encapsulate the incredible impact and the importance of programs like these throughout American correctional institutions.

In the early 1970s Dr. Elizabeth "Ma" Barker, professor of English at Boston University became involved in the debate club at MCI-Norfolk, a medium-security men's prison in Norfolk, MA. In these intercollegiate debate tournaments the men at Norfolk defeated several debate teams from different universities including Harvard and MIT. Barker noted the incredible intellect and potential of the men at Norfolk and set out to create a prison education program. From this idea, she founded the Boston University Prison Education Program (BUPEP) in 1972, with the goal of giving students an opportunity to advance their education and in turn lower recidivism rates.[1]

Since its founding, the BU Prison Education Program has offered different degrees and lost funding from the federal government. In spite of these obstacles it has stayed true to its mission. Now privately funded through Boston University alone, the BU Prison Education Program continues for undergraduate education encouraged mostly by low recidivism rates among its graduates who are released.

Although these numbers are not available for BU PEP, similar programs such as Hudson Link report a 0% recidivism rate. This low recidivism rate is true for students who participate in post-secondary education programs across the U.S. The correlation between education programs and recidivism rates is well-documented.[2] This paper aims to demonstrate that post-secondary education is a valuable investment for the Department of Corrections since post-secondary education programs help meet the goals of correctional institutions such as rehabilitation and behavioral correction. Post-secondary education requires students to think critically, reflect on their vocation, and affords graduates favorable job prospects after their release.

Reflecting on one's vocation and goals is an important skill for someone who has transgressed social laws; they must be able to think of what they want to do differently once they are released. Without proper reflection and acquisition of credentials there is a higher incidence of recidivism. Programs such as the BU Prison Education Program are essential, otherwise, we as a society are warehousing people without allowing them to improve themselves, or to gain a sense of purpose and maintain their human dignity. In the past, warehousing people has proved more costly and detrimental to corrections departments. Through the history of American punishment, there is both an urge to punish as well as an impetus to rehabilitate. Scholars have referred to this as a policy pendulum.' In the 1990s when the pendulum swung to stop post-secondary correctional programs, recidivism only increased.

This paper aims to provide evidence for the positive influence the BU PEP has had on current students and its importance as the objective of rehabilitation. The Massachusetts Department of Corrections uses the term "rehabilitation" to denote how the services the DOC provides will enable individuals to return to their communities as law-abiding citizens. The Massachusetts Department of Corrections (MDOC) defines rehabilitation as an environment designed to "eliminate violence, victimization and recidivism."[4] I argue that post-secondary education meets the goals and objectives toward the rehabilitation of individuals that the MDOC has under its care and custody.

The purpose of this paper is three-fold, it will (1) contextualize the BU PEP within larger national trends of post-secondary education, (2) present the voices of current BU students at MCI-Norfolk, whose words will reflect on the impact of the program, (3) give recommendations for implementing post-secondary education more widely and make BU PEP more effective.

I was driven to conduct this research because of my experiences as a student in one BU PEP course. During the course I sought to understand the impact that this program has had on my classmates' time in prison since they were nothing like the ontological other I had imagined before enrolling in this course, I was able to see that they were different people from the ones who first came through the prison doors. My BU classmates are engaged and critical thinkers that seek to improve not only themselves but also the community around them. The impetus behind this research is to provide additional evidence for the positive impact that post-secondary prison education programs have both inside and outside prison walls (namely its impact on recidivism rates), in so doing I hope to show that we need to adopt post-secondary education programs more widely across the U.S.

A Brief History of Post-Secondary Prison Education Programs in the U.S.

Post-secondary prison education programs are programs that seek to address factors that contribute to incarceration and assist with reintegration into society by providing credit and non-credit college-level courses to students before their release from prison. Although this definition includes distance learning, I will only focus on on-site instruction and classes that are able to create a community of learners, since this is the nature of the BU PEP. Post-secondary prison education programming is part of "correctional services ... essentially strategic interventions designed to assist inmates with specific needs, and to maintain organization and structure within the constraints of a correctional setting."[6]

After the Attica rebellion of 1971, in Attica New York, Attica Correctional Facility at the time was overcrowded almost to double its capacity, men there were denied basic hygienic supplies and there were no programs available. Prisoners sought to make demands, which were not heard by the state government, the rebellion ended in a massacre that left 43 people dead. One of the demands made by the men who organized this rebellion was to have better rehabilitative programs.[7]

After this massacre, which brought national attention to the human rights violations and deplorable conditions of American prisons, prison education programs became widely implemented across American correctional institutions. The focus of American correctional institutions in the 1970s and 1980s was geared toward rehabilitation. In the 1990s, a punitive approach to corrections resurfaced in correctional policies. In 1992, Governor of Massachusetts William F. Weld addressed an audience at the Attorney General's Summit on Corrections, he stated, "I'm of the belief that prison should be like a tour though the circles of hell. In making it so, however, our task is a formidable one since we have to undo many years in which Massachusetts treated crime as a social services matter rather than a public safety problem"[10]

This attitude toward correctional institutions was not unique to Massachusetts; in fact it was a national shift. In 1994, Congress passed The Crime Control Act, severely limiting the funding of post-secondary prison education programs. The rationale was that prisons had become country clubs, with too many amenities; funneling Pell grant funding to people who had been convicted of crimes was taking away money from law-abiding citizens.

Criminologist Joshua Searcy explains the effects that the bill had, "Congress made convicted felons ineligible for Pell grants, the federal tuition aid program aimed primarily at the poor. The government also limited the flow of money to prisons for adult and special education-a move that turned out to be seriously self- destructive."[11] In naming this political move self-destructive, Searcy understands that lack of funding for educational programs in prison led to higher recidivism rates, higher incarceration and more broken communities.

This policy shift in the federal government affected the BU PEP and other college programs that were offering classes in conjunction with the BU PEP. In 1985, the BU PEP had begun granting master's degrees in interdisciplinary studies. Local community colleges were teaching the general distribution courses and Boston University was teaching concentration and graduate-level courses. However, due to lack of funding and because other local community colleges were not able to continue teaching in prisons, Boston University had to re-structure its program to offer both general education requirements and higher level courses. The BU PEP after 1994 was under-staffed and could no longer offer a master's program.[12]

Since 1997, BU PEP partnered with the organization Partakers[13] in order to provide BU students with a connection to the outside world by pairing them with mentor volunteers who keep in contact with them. In the past, students had to obtain enough college credits from another college in order to transfer them to BU. Since 1994, accruing those credits from other community colleges became more difficult, and taking correspondence courses could be costly. BU found that qualified men were not in the program because they could not afford correspondence courses. To address this issue, now BU allows students to take an entrance exam in order to be enrolled.

Impact of Boston University Prison Education Program on Students at MCI- Norfolk

There are currently 82 undergraduate students enrolled in the BU program at MCI-Norfolk. Their racial make up consists of 51 % White, 23% Black, 17% Hispanic, 6% Asian. There are also 28 students who are graduates of BU and audit one course each semester; their racial breakdown is similar to that of the undergraduate students. BU students at Norfolk are also different ages and at different points in their sentences. The sample of BU student reflections I was able to obtain are from 15 students from diverse racial backgrounds, at different parts of the program.[14] The form that was distributed to BU students had one question, "How has going to BU impacted your life?"[15] Some of the practical reasons for implementing a program like BU PEP is obvious: it will allow people who are currently incarcerated to be more prepared to enter the job marked upon release because they will have more credentials.

Better credentials are not all a post-secondary prison education program enables an individual to accomplish. The importance and value of prison education go well-beyond employment. "Reading, writing and thinking allows many ex-offenders to reflect on their actions instead of living on impulse."[16] If a person is not only able to have better credentials for employment but also able to reflect on the harms he inflicted on society, post-secondary education serves two important purposes of rehabilitation, addressing victimization and stopping the cycle of recidivism. Some of the themes that this section will explore through student reflections are how BU increases students' confidence, allows them to develop meaningful relationships and gives students productive goals to work toward.

African American student Jeffrey,[17] who is only in his second semester at BU has found confidence and improvements in his self-esteem through the program. He writes,

Greatings [sic] Fellow Americans,

Thank you for asking me to participate in this project. I am now in my second semester of the B.U. program at M.C.I Norfolk and the changes that are manifesting in my life due to the program are nothing short of miraculas [sic]. Words can't express the gratitude I feel towards God, Mass. D.O.C, and all the staff that make the B.U. program a reality. I know that I wouldn't be able to achieve a bachelors degree without being in a structured environment like M.C.I Norfolk, so I am very greatful [sic] to the classification department of the Mass. D.O.C., as well.

I am in awe of what I have learned in just two semesters. If you told me just one year ago, that I would be calculating algebra, trigonometry and statistics; that I would be analyzing the works of Shakespeare, and writing B+ grade worthy English essays, I would've told you, "Aha right, you're out of your mind." The biggest impact that this program is having on me is bettering my self esteem, which is giving me a new perspective on what I can do with the rest of my life. Helping myself and helping others with my experiences and what I am now learning in the BU Program.

Juan is a Latino student and sophomore in the program, he writes about his experience in the BU prison education program,

First, you should know that I'm the guy covered in tattoos whom you can't help but pass judgment on. Growing up my mother was addicted to heroin, and my father remains a mystery to me. English is still my second language and ignorance has been everything I could have imagined but bliss. As I write this I turn 31 and I'm faced with the reality that I have spent more time incarcerated than living a full life. Even behind bars my life mainly consisted of: drinking, smoking, fighting, and selling drugs. Basically, my life has had no purpose, no goal, and therefore, no achievements. Yet, a man without a purpose is a man with no identity, no religion or conviction and thus lacks the ability to be a man under any condition.

Boston University has become the Peter of my church, the rock on which I build the foundation of my newfound religion (education). It has given me what I always needed; direction, guidance and purpose. I now seek to achieve both, short and long term goals, as well as build rather than destroy. It has taught me how to be a leader, but most importantly it is still teaching me how to think for myself. For the first time in my life I think about the consequences of my actions, and I appreciate something so much that I fear losing it. I finally understand why to whom much is given to, much is required of, or why any faith without works is death.

Boston University has not only taught me the importance of critical thinking, but also how to commit myself and apply the work that is necessary to not just speak about, but to be about a more positive cause. In short, what Boston University has done is change my perspective on life and thereby changed me.

As it is clear from Juan's reflection his entire orientation to life has changed. The perspective this program has given him strikes me because of the confidence it has given him to create a better future for himself. Juan also mentions the privilege that participating in BU PEP is and will avoid any conduct violation in order to continue their education.

People are not only transformed in their character when they can learn and think critically. Prison education also appears to "increase the safety of the corrections officers because men and women inmates are productively occupied while incarcerated and recruit other prisoners to the program."[18] Having programs with dedicated educators that foster community helps the individuals improve themselves and is not only good for the person who is incarcerated but for correctional officers and communities at large.

A young white student, Richard, also speaks about how much the program means to him and how he wouldn't want to jeopardize it,

There is so much I could say. This program has transformed my life on so many fronts. In the end-I graduate in a month or two-BU has been the catalyst I needed to become a more responsible, focused man. Through working with other students who, quite honestly, I would have probably never talked to before school, I was able to free myself from the harmful social barriers that I promoted. Having the BU professors come in here endure the systems that frustrate them, and still treat me like a human being who actually matters in the world counterbalances the dehumanizing effects of institutionalization that works so hard to consume me. The work load keeps the wheels of progress moving by constantly challenging my ability and way of thinking. I could go on for some time. However, BU has made me a serious personal impact on me in a very personal way. You see, before prison I used drugs to numb emotions that were uncomfortable in my life. In prison, and without a regular supply of drugs, those emotions were calmed by violence, anger and aggression. Once I was given the opportunity to go to college-faced with all the aesthetic benefits-I was forced to deal with emotions in a more positive way something I haven't done completely my whole life-or I would lose the opportunity to go to school.

My journey was not easy. I have challenges that others do not, it seems, in terms of processing emotions. The progress I have made over the past five years has given me so much strength. Not to take anything away from the education itself, it's just that having something so important that I could lose in the blink of an eye should I react to negativity the wrong way or allow, what have now become much more familiar emotions, to find an outlet in anger, I would lose everything. Because of this BU has transformed my life and my future.

Richard's mention of the importance of community like classmates, professors and mentors is important because a relational ethic comes alive in education: people are healed in relationship with each other. People do not flourish in isolation but when forming supportive relationships. In a conversation I had with him, he expressed to me that he appreciates BU PEP more than any other program in prison because in this program, unlike others offered at Norfolk, those in power treat him with respect and integrity. They do not feel sorry for him and they expect excellence from him.

An African American student named Joshua names interactions with classmates and professors "therapeutic."

Class and study times force me to interact with others, and I have found
this to be at the least therapeutic, and in many ways has given me back
my sense of humanity. I have hope again and am beginning to believe in
myself once more.

In a paramilitary environment such as prison, where fear and violence
are the norm, the classroom functions as a safe space to be in relationship
with each other. Theologian T. Richard Snyder notes about Ubuntu ethics,
"A person is human precisely in being enveloped in the community of other
human beings, in being caught up in the bundle of life."[19] Relationships are
integral in healing and regenerating, post-secondary education programs
create important communities that are essential in gaining new perspectives.

Although students in this sample did not mention it directly, the
organization Partakers, through its program College Behind Bars, plays an
important role by connecting a person in BU PEP with a community
member to correspond and visit, a way to keep a connection to the outside
and encourage students to continue pursuing their degree. This one-on-one
mentoring has been effective and crucial for transformation for both, the
mentors and the mentees.[20]

Boston University alumnus and graduate of BU PEP, Thomas, is a
middle age white man who found his career path by being exposed to great
works of literature during his tenure as a student. He writes in his reflection,

I attended the BU PEP from the fall of 2008 to the spring of 2013. I
graduated with a 3.88 GPA which allowed me the honor of being my class's
valedictorian. In my speech, I pointed out how education breaks the chains
(both physical and meta-physical) that binds us, and that is exactly what BU
did for me-especially in three areas: my goals, my health, and my role.

Throughout my life I have been an avid reader, however through BU I have realized that I want to create stories as well as read them. By taking several writing courses, I have discovered that I have a gift for writing fiction (as well as poetry), and it has become a goal of mine to become a published writer. Without BU, I would have never contemplated such an idea. One particular class changed my life completely. It was a class on nutrition. Because of this class, I have lost around 70 pounds, and have learned the importance of counting calories in order to have a balanced and healthy life. I am in better shape now at the age of 42 than I was at age 25. All because of having my eyes opened (through education) to see how unhealthy I was and the lame excuses I used to justify it.

The BU PEP has allowed me to be a role-model for my son, and that is the biggest role I have in my life. The day before my graduation, he wrote on the chalkboard in his classroom that he would not be in school the next day because he would be attending my graduation.

My wife told me that he was proud of me for being the valedictorian, but the best part-for me-was being able to tell him via my speech that he inspired me not only to be a better student but a better man as well.

I will be eternally grateful to BU for this program. It has given me the ability and courage to go through life the best way I can-and that is to never stop learning in order to keep any chains from binding me.

Thomas' newfound career is one of the most important aspects of his time in BU PEP. Relationships also figure prominently in his narrative, as he was able to become a role model for his son. Children with a parent behind bars are more likely to go to prison in her/his lifetime. Michel Foucault contends, "the prison indirectly produces delinquents by throwing the inmate's family into destitution."[21] However, I believe programs like BU PEP have the power to reduce the likelihood of children of incarcerated parents going to prison. Given the accomplishments of Thomas, it is very unlikely that his son will be incarcerated. Thomas' perspective and experiences will prove valuable to rearing his son and guiding him to make appropriate decisions.

Recommendations for Post-Secondary Prison Education Programs

If the main function of prisons is to rehabilitate those who are convicted, then current correctional institutions are abysmally failing in this regard. Post-secondary education is an important avenue for rehabilitation. The U.S. makes up 5% of the global population, yet houses 25% of the world's prisoners. In addition, we have stunningly high recidivism rates, precisely because our system fails to rehabilitate those who have broken laws and transgressed moral norms. Programs such as the Boston University Prison Education Program are essential in providing people under custody humane treatment, and it is a cheap alternative to housing someone after they re-offend. The cost of one year of BUPEP is $1,800.[22] which is a fraction of the price of housing a man at Norfolk, which is $34,996.23 Post-secondary prison education programs offer a caring, comparatively cheap and effective alternative to the discipline-and-punish ideology that has pervaded correctional institutions.[24] This approach breeds only hopelessness in the lives of those behind bars, exacerbating the rates of recidivism.

As it is clear from student reflections the Boston University Prison Education Program is incredibly valuable and is committed to providing a quality education to the men at Norfolk. Current BU students and BU graduates are often eager to help others attain a college degree, they tutor prospective students who are preparing to take the entrance exam. A formal mentoring program would be enriching for students to have more of a community and to be able to build relationships with each other in a mentoring context.

In addition, many college programs have career counseling available which I believe would enhance the BUPEP, students would be able to reflect on what they would like to do upon release and get connected to resources, agencies and non- profits that would be helpful to BU graduates who have a criminal record. More support especially in transitioning back to the home community would be helpful to make the most of the BU degree.

Conclusions

In this paper I have argued that postsecondary prison education programs are necessary if correctional institutions are going to take their task to rehabilitate individuals seriously.[25] Many of those who arrive in prison never received educational opportunities equal to those of their peers. Post-secondary prison education programs do more than impart knowledge of philosophy or statistics. The stories of the BU Prison Education students show that they have been able to find their voice, and feel like their voices are heard. BU students who pursue their degree while incarcerated gain confidence and become thoughtful and reflective. Education in prison has a transformative impact in a way that people on the outside may not be able to appreciate. For many people in the U.S. from certain class and racial backgrounds, education was a given as people who commit crimes, especially related to drug charges such as possession or intent to sell are likely to come from poor neighborhoods with failing school systems. Prison houses women and men who were never given a chance to become critical thinkers or encouraged to further their education and make a better life for themselves. A current BU student, Martin, wrote, "So many of these men need confidence. It's a self-perpetuating reality that they're not smart, they've been made to feel that way." Many of the men at Norfolk came from communities with social problems such as drug abuse, gun violence and poverty as it is clear from their writings.

To this point, scholar and prison educator Kaia Stern estimates, "the vast majority of people are imprisoned for non-violent, drug-related offenses, have less than a ninth-grade education, and were born and raised in communities of concentrated disadvantage."[26]

Education is a powerful tool, it allows people to reflect on the harm they have caused society. Post-secondary education programs are an important rehabilitation strategy to maintain in prisons because they have proven not only incredibly effective in reducing recidivism but as this paper shows, people's perspectives change and thereby so does their behavior in and outside of prison. Prison educator Matthew Spellberg, who teaches comparative literature in New Jersey notes, "Education is not the only avenue toward recovering and protecting one's dignity in prison, but it is a major one, done right, it offers a modicum of the authority required of a person for self-creation: It makes a person in some modest way master of his or her own mind."[27]

Former Massachusetts Governor, William F. Weld pointed out that prisons should primarily function to deter offenders from engaging in criminal activities, and that it is simply ludicrous for their purpose to be focused on helping the individual through social services. The evidence I have presented in this paper shows that describing it as an issue of public safety vs. individual social services is a false dichotomy. As a society can do both; we can continue to fund prisons as a way to deter people from committing crimes but also make their time in prison productive, by providing them with appropriate rehabilitative programs that in turn prevent recidivism. In doing so, we are putting both public safety and individual needs at the forefront of correctional institutional policy. It is not only the more humane approach to corrections but also the more fiscally responsible.

I would like to end this paper by highlighting a conversation that three of my classmates had while thinking about prison reform and what needs to change in the correctional system,

> A: In my view, education is the tool, what we most need in this world.

> B: I volunteer in the BU Prep program, I tutor them in reading or math. You just see their confidence go up, like aw man, I can do algebra!

> C: Tutoring, that's the price we pay, there's no tuition but that's the price we pay!

These men are not only thinking of themselves anymore. They encourage and help each other to attain a bachelor's degree. I believe that is a true testament to the kind of transformative experience that the BU program has had on the lives of these students. We often hear in the American political arena that we need to place public safety first and helping individuals second; post-secondary prison education programs allows correctional institutions to do both. Education will save tax-payer money and allow individuals and communities to flourish. It is irresponsible and incongruent with Massachusetts Department of Corrections philosophy to deny people opportunities to improve themselves and become transformed by knowledge through education.

I would like to thank everyone who made this research possible by sharing their experiences with me. I would also like to acknowledge one of my classmates in particular who helped me collect the data and gave me feedback on his own experiences in the BU program. I hope I have represented them accurately and respectfully. I am inspired by each of you. Thank you.

Appendix A

The questionnaire that BU students at Norfolk were given asked them about their experiences on the BU PEP as well as some key words to orient their thinking.

Thank you so much for participating in this project!

Question: How has going to BU impacted your life?

Share as much as you are comfortable with while striving to demonstrate how these changes have manifested in your life.

Some key words to consider are:

Behavior-Attitude-Perspective-Health-Faith-Direction-Growth.

If you could also include how long you've been with the program that would also be helpful.

Endnotes

1. Boston University Prison Education Program website, http://www.bu.edu/pep/about us/
2. See 2013 RAND, "Evaluating the Effectiveness of Correctional Education," Steurer "Education Reduces Crime: Recidivism Study, Three State Summary," and "The Top Nine Reasons to Increase Correctional Education Programs," Erisman and Contardo "Learning to Reduce Recidivism: A state analysis of postsecondary correctional education policy," Sherman, "Preventing Crime: What Works, What Doesn't, What's Promising,"
3. I borrow this term from Religion scholar Kaia Stern who notes that correctional policies usually operate on a pendulum. Throughout the history of punishment in the U.S. there has been a tendency to punish and to rehabilitate.
4. Massachusetts Department of Correction, http://www.mass.gov/eopss/agencies/doc/ Although I resist the word rehabilitation, because it necessarily labels people as delinquents and in need of institutionalized compulsory help, it is dehumanizing. As Michel Foucault points out by labeling people as delinquents or people in special need of rehabilitation, it is perpetuating delinquency itself. However, I use rehabilitation because it is the language used by correctional institutions to attempt to modify people's behavior, in doing so I hope to demonstrate that done right, "rehabilitation" can occur in prison particularly through post-secondary education programs.
5. Jeanne Contardo and Michelle Tolbert, "Prison Postsecondary Education: Bridging Learning from Incarceration to the Community," 1-15, 2008. http://www.urban.org/projects/reentry- roundtable/upload /Contardo.pdf
6 Joshua Searcy, Correctional Education, Program Services and Inmate Recidivism: Education Programs and Services/or Inmates (Saarbriiken: VDM Verlag, 2009),75
7. Jan Buruma, "Uncaptive Minds" February 20, 2005. The New York Times. http://select.nvtimes.com/gst/abstract.html?res=FA0914F93ESEOC738ED DAB089400404-482
8. Donald A. Jelinek. Attica justice: The Cruel 30-year legacy of the nation's bloodiest prison rebellion, which transformed the American Prison System (Jelinek Publishers, 2011), 1-10.
9. In this speech he addressed the way in which he sought to cut spending for prisons and how to make them less comfortable and instead for them to fulfill their "true" purpose of punishing people.
10. Remarks by the Governor William F. Weld, The Attorney General's Summit on Corrections Monday April 27, 1992, Washington D.C.

11. Brent Staples,"Prison Class: What Ma Barker Knew that Congress Didn't," November 25, 2002, Editorial Observer, The New York Times. www.nytimes.com/2002/.11L25LQ12inion/e_cjJto_rigJ:. observer-prison-class-what-ma-barker-knew-and-congress-didn-t.html
12. Conversation with Robert Cadigan, past director of the Boston University Prison Education Program.
14. Boston University Prison Education Program Document, "Racial Breakdown of Active Students"
15. For a sample form see Appendix A.
16. David Skorton and Glenn Altschuler, "College Behind Bars: How Educating Prisoners Pays Off' March 25, 2013. Forbes Magazine http://www.forbcs.com/sitesLcollegeprose/2013/03/25/college behind-bars-how-educating-prisoners-pays-off/
17. All the names and any identifying characteristics of all students presented in this paper have been changed to protect their privacy.
18. David Skorton and Glenn Altschuler, "College Behind Bars: How Educating Prisoners Pays Off' March 25, 2013. Forbes Magazine http://www.forbcs.com/sitesLcollegeprose/2013/03/25/college behind-bars-how-educating-prisoners-pays-off/
19. T. Richard Snyder, The Protestant Ethic and the Spirit of Punishment (Grand Rapids, MI: Wm. B. Eerdmans Publishing Co), 2001, 106.
20. Partakers, College Behind Bars website, http://partakers.org/site/college-behind-barsl
21. Michel Foucault, Discipline and Punish (New York, NY: Vintage Books, znd Edition) translated by Alan Sheridan, 268.
22. Figure obtained from a conversation with former BU PEP director Robert Cadigan.
23. Statistic as of 2010, "Massachusetts Department of Corrections Prison Population Trends Report" http:// II www. bostonarearesea rchinitiative.net/assets/prison-pop-trends-2010%281%29 .pdf
24. David Skorton and Glenn Altschuler, "College Behind Bars: How Educating Prisoners Pays Off' March 25, 2013. Forbes Magazine http://www.forbcs.com/sitesLcollegeprose/2013/03/25/college behind-bars-how-educating-prisoners-pays-off/
26. Kaia Stern, "Shackles and Sunlight" Fellowship of Reconciliation: Working for peace, non-violence and reconciliation since 1915. http://forusa.org/fellowship/2011/springshackles-sunlight/12654 Stern also notes that many people in prison may be functionally illiterate and have been passed through the public school system.
27. David Skorton and Glenn Altschuler, "College Behind Bars: How Educating Prisoners Pays Off' March 25, 2013. Forbes Magazine. http://www.forbes.com/sites/collegeprose/2013/03/25/college behind-bars-how-educating-prisoners-pays-off/

The Act of Guilt Performativity in the Justice System

Jennifer Hernandez

The film *The Shawshank Redemption* based on the book Rita Hayworth and Shawshank Redemption by Stephen King is the story in which "Two imprisoned men bond over a number of years, finding solace and eventual redemption through acts of common decency".[1] A film about a particular experience in the prison system which serves as an example of the way in which the prison system works. The film reflects many characteristics of life in prison, and has been among one of the critically acclaimed films on its topic. One scene in particular from this film that struck me when I first watched it was that concerning a parole hearing.

The film opens with Red, one of the main characters confronting his parole hearing after serving 20 years of his life sentence and getting asked the question: "Do you feel you have been rehabilitated?", and Red answering "Oh yes, sir absolutely sir, I mean I learned my lesson. I can honestly say that I'm a changed man. I'm no longer a danger to society".[2] This same procedure happens one more time within a timeframe of ten years, and ends with similar answers. On both counts Red gets denied parole, although it seems as if he was saying exactly what the parole board wanted to hear. Finally, on the third time after ten more years (for a total of forty years in prison) he confronts the process once again but this time is approved for parole. There is a major change in his attitude and answers to the parole board, one would not give him a great chance to be granted parole in real life, I believe; "stop wasting my time. Because to tell you the truth, I don't give a shit."[3]

The process of parole experienced through the character Red seems to be incomprehensible, and unapproachable because there are no set definitions on the expectations. The goal of a parole hearing has the purpose of making sure the person convicted for the crime communicates regret and the feeling of repentance. These characteristics are a requirement in order to demonstrate "rehabilitation" (although this part is not made explicit in the laws or expectations put forward officially by the Commonwealth of Massachusetts). The term "rehabilitation" is a constant part of not only the decisions of parole hearings but the criminal justice systems' jails and prisons. The reason for incarceration is to punish while a second goal is to "rehabilitate". However, some offenders are deemed unable to be rehabilitated based on the crime they have committed when they are convicted and sentenced, for these people parole is just a re-affirmation from the criminal system that they have no chance at redemption. The general idea of being "rehabilitated'" entails no longer being a threat to society, by this the criminal justice system expects the parolee to not commit any more crimes. How this is interpreted by each of the parole members during a hearing is particular to what each considers a sign of this rehabilitation, and the first step to grant parole is to believe that an offender can in fact be rehabilitated. Since parole hearings and cases are approached individually, some offenders can be granted parole. The parole board in the Commonwealth of Massachusetts officially defines its purpose as; "We have primary responsibility of identifying those parole eligible offenders for whom there is sufficient indications that confinement has served its purpose, but others are not even considered rehabilitable setting appropriate conditions for parole, and enhancing public safety through the responsible reintegration of these individuals to the community".[5] However, there is no official definition of what a parole hearing, is what the parole board intends to witness, or what the goals of a parole hearing are in regards to the return of "offenders" to society. I argue that these hearings that lead to the rejection or approval of parole have as a purpose the search for repentance of the person who has committed the crime, and is based on the sole credibility of the case presented to the parole board. This faulty system has a in base the requirement of the acceptance of guilt for the crime committed in order to obtain freedom on parole even if innocent of the crime convicted of. With our faulty criminal justice system, that often targets specific groups based on race and socioeconomic status, and sometimes even incarcerates innocent people, this approach results in more problems than solutions.

Rehabilitation, repentance, and regret for wrong doings are elements that are part of the goal of parole hearings and the criminal justice system at large. However, it seems illogical to be able to measure these feelings quantitatively in any situation. Is it realistically possible to measure these characteristics in a person, and who can be in charge of such arbitrary decisions? This form of judgment seems to be one that feeds to a "God complex" in which the members of a parole board and, more extensively, the criminal justice system have the power to decide if someone is redeemable and worth saving, or who will be saved. T. Richard Snyder in his book *The Protestant Ethic and the Spirit of Punishment* presents the argument of the creation of the "other", which makes it easier to see a separation of "offenders" and the rest of the population. With this idea we seek to maintain the "other" away from the rest of society and the differences between "us" and "they" makes punishment a necessary and unquestioned reaction to crime. Authorities have the power to decide who this "other" group is and whether "they" can ever be part of the "us" again; "While Yahweh may have said, "Vengeance is mine, I will repay," it would seem that our society either considers itself God or has concluded that God's promise is vacuous. What we do to those we incarcerate suggests that our soul is cold to the point of death".[6] Parole and parole hearings were first introduced as a middle ground in which this "other", previously unredeemable and condemned to death for the offenses committed was for the first time thought to have some characteristics that might give them the chance to rejoin the "us" in the larger society.

The term and concept of "Parole" was a response to a change in perspective of authorities towards people who committed a crime; "Reform became fashionable and from the ecclesiastical prison tradition of the Middle Ages the concept emerged that, perhaps, the offender might be worth saving. Prisons came to be regarded as places of contemplation, repentance, meditation and expiation".[7] The beginning of the pursuit of people who had committed crimes was for the purpose of essentially getting rid of them. The general idea was that criminals were innately bad and there was no way to change this, so the only way to prevent the recurrence of crime was to get rid of these people. The change in this mentality took place at the turn of the late 18th and early 19th century, where the variety of crimes increased and many of these were deemed not sufficiently serious to require automatic death sentences as a form of punishment.

The first models of prison-like institutions served as a temporary place in which to host the captured criminals until they were executed. Some of the first recorded examples of this change and laws that backed up the change of authorities assumptions were presented in New York during the year 1877 under what was known as "indeterminate sentences".[8] During these sentences a judge issued a minimum amount of time that the person convicted would serve, but this judge did not set a maximum time to be served. The convicted person would go through a sort of retrial after this minimum time was served, in which reformation was expected for the purpose of proving rehabilitation. During this time the person imprisoned would participate in programs, learn crafts and be graded by the board of the prison, this board had the power to set the person free or deem them incapable to be returned to society. If they decided that the person imprisoned was not fit to leave the prison the board had the power to decide the maximum time the person would be in captivity based on the behavior they had witnessed. These indeterminate sentences could last a lifetime ending in death of natural causes, but while still in prison.

When examining the approach in a parole hearing that serves to judge the person already convicted of a crime this time around to judge whether the person has been rehabilitated, there are obviously only two ways to look at the situation, and only two possible outcomes. The person incarcerated is either found worthy of salvation or doomed; "The indeterminate sentence pointed in two directions: leniency and rehabilitation for the savable; eternal damnation for the rest".[9]

Although the change to this type of system and mentality from that of thinking that those who committed crimes would eternally be a threat to society was a good step towards a more just system and seemed to be a comprehensible way to move away from the idea of the "habitual criminal". The pre-imposed assumptions that the parole board makes based on the crime committed by a person already convicted hold too much weight. The parole board can, and many times do, base their verdicts on the magnitude of the crime and makes the connection between it and the idea of rehabilitation, coming to the conclusion that some crimes are so bad that the person who has committed them cannot possibly be able to reach rehabilitation. This way of thinking is an extension of the pre-18th century period, when this way of thinking is argued to have changed. The habitual criminal was thought to continuously commit more crimes if let free, and the only way to end the cycle was through death. The idea of the habitual criminal continued, while being partially masked by the new procedure of paroles, but people incarcerated are still serving life sentences that lead to death in prison, with parole being an illusion. Only a small percentage of the population was seen as redeemable through parole. The possibility of parole carried on the opportunity to obtain redemption. This is especially true in the cases of life sentences; these can be given by the judge with or without the possibility of parole. The people convicted and sentenced to life without parole have already been deemed as damned and without the possibility to be "saved", forgiven, or part of the regular society as citizens.

The rest of those sentenced to life with the possibility of parole hang on a thread where they are considered to have some redeeming qualities but are applied "indeterminate sentences" which might not end until death; "Parole was a way to correct for inequities in sentencing. More importantly, it was still another way to sift worthy from unworthy prisoners, and give the worthy ones a chance to prove themselves."[10] Parole was an alternative to death, but in the case of those given life without parole this does not serve that purpose. Parole is still stemmed from the idea that the person convicted is a "habitual criminal" that will continue to commit offenses if they are not "rehabilitated". This way of thinking is especially, if not only, found with offenders who are sentenced to large amounts of time in prison such as twenty or more years, like is the example with "lifers". Those who are in prison for shorter periods of time don't have to prove whether they are "rehabilitated", or answer questions as to whether they are sorry for whatever crime they have committed.

In modernity for someone to be considered for parole, that is to have a hearing: which does not guarantee the granting of parole, they need to have served the minimum sentence prescribed by the judge or a third of their sentence. The years that need to be served before being eligible to apply for parole vary by decision of the judge, and state regulations. The decision to grant parole is described by the United States Department of Justice to be based on the following statement; "When someone is paroled they serve part of their sentence under the supervision of their community. The law says that the U.S. Parole Commission may grant parole if (a) the inmate has substantially observed the rules of the institution; (b) release would not depreciate the seriousness of the offense or promote disrespect for the law; and (c) release would not jeopardize the public welfare".[11] These are in the standards that are in place in order to be considered apt to go back to the larger society but still under the watch of the law. Convicted offenders have to be on the further end of rehabilitation to be granted parole.

The idea of being "rehabilitated" is a creation of the change of approach to the belief that criminals were not innately criminal or bad people, before this change there was no belief that rehabilitation was possible. However, using this term "rehabilitation" can be problematic, because there is no set standard on what rehabilitation looks like. For this purpose I have chosen to use the Massachusetts law regarding parole hearings and decision making, which gives us some insight into what a common ground on the definition of rehabilitation might look like based on the reasons of the board to grant or deny parole after the hearings;

"Parole Board Members shall only grant a parole permit if they are of the opinion that there is a reasonable probability that, if such offender is released, the offender will live and remain at liberty without violating the law and that release is not incompatible with the welfare of society. Parole Board Members shall not grant a parole permit merely as a reward for good institutional conduct. M.G.L. c. 127, § 130".[12]

In reviewing the decisions of parole hearings for people who were sentenced to life with the possibility of parole for the years 2011-2014, 2013 is the first year in which this description on the grounds by which to grant parole starts appearing on every single official document of the hearings.[13] Whether the convicted person has been granted, or denied parole this same text appears as the justification for the decision. The decision is fully up to the parole board members in every case and although there is a thread on what the parole members take into account to grant the parole such as participation in programs offered, dealing with the motives that led them to commit their crime e.g. anger management, therapy, etc., which aid in the demonstration of repentance. The process of the hearing is in addition particularly shaped by the history; the recollection of the crime committed and the acknowledgement of guilt. Other factors include the input and views of the public, in some cases the testifying of the victim or family of the victim and even D.O.C officers.

In decisions of parole hearings for lifers in the Commonwealth of Massachusetts the decision of the parole board are influenced by not just the hearing and the behavior of the person incarcerated but with all associated with the case and crime. An example of a decision of a lifer reads as follows:

> **DECISION OF THE BOARD**: After careful consideration of all relevant facts including the nature of the underlying offense, criminal record, institutional record, the inmate's testimony at the hearing, and the view of the public as expressed at the hearing or in writing, we conclude by unanimous vote that the inmate .....[14]

This piece of text is present in all the latest reports of hearings available to the public from 2013 up to the most recent decisions available. There is an attempt to explain with greater clarity the way in which decisions are made by the parole board that is reflected in parole hearing statements starting in 2013. Before this there was no mention of the elements that came to affect the decision of the board, there was simply a "Parole is denied" or "Parole is approved" as part of a two-page report. In comparison to this, the report from 2013 and on are much more detailed containing the factors taken into account, a recounting of the crime committed and the process that resulted in incarceration, the history of the person's case in the prison system and previous accounts of parole hearings if this is not the first one.

In a report about the "Parole Decisions for Lifers" put together by a group called "Norfolk Lifers Group" in the year 2013 (the most recent report coming on the issue from this group) we can find a section attributed to the "Approval factors" in parole hearings for lifers in the Commnonwealth of

Massachusetts. These factors have been found to be the most significant when approving the granting of parole, even though every case has its own particularities the factors were the ones that were seen more repeatedly and in more combinations of those who obtained paroles. For this year (2013) it was reported that 137 parole hearings took place but only 21 (15.3%) of these were approved to parole.[15]

The top five frequency percentages go as follow:

1. Active Program participation   71.4% (15of 21)

2. Four goals of punishment met   52.4% (11 of 21)
    (punishment, deterrence, public protection and rehabilitation)

3. No risk for future violent acts   47.6% (10 of21)

4. Steady employment while incarcerated   47.6% (10 of21)

5. High level of community support   47.6% (10 of21)[16]

In this list there is a clear emphasis put on program participation that correlates to the granting of parole. It is advised by the authorities in prison to participate in programs, which help to resolve the root of the crime committed. To know what programs to approach is to accept that you have committed that crime and are willing to work to resolve the issues within yourself and the things that triggered that event; the offender has to repent and make amends through the programs first. "Lifers approved for paroles were those who had successfully addressed their areas of need, e.g., substance abuse, violence, anger and then were able to explain convincingly what they had learned, how the programs had changed their lives for better, and that they no longer pose a threat to the welfare of society".[17] However even though program participation is so important to acquire parole

Massachusetts general laws Chapter 127, Section 130 explicitly mention that parole should not be granted solely on program participation." In the report the author/s notice a very interesting and specific detail that has been made less explicit but matches the idea that repentance, regret and the acceptance of responsibility are needed to even be considered for a parole hearing, to be considered worth saving;

> As with 2011/2012, five approval factors utilized by the Parole Board in 2009 and 2010 that were distinctly absent in 2013. These were: Accepts Responsibility, Expresses Remorse, Family support, Solid Parole Plan, and understands Causative Factors of criminal behavior. Their absence suggests that the present Parole Board expects that those factors will be addressed by the lifer as a minimum to receive and serious consideration from a possible parole and, therefore, need not be given special recognition. Not having adequately addressed one or more of these five factors, however, is a sure path to denial.[19]

Although denial or better yet the admission of guilt should not be a factor that would influence a parole hearing based on policy, there are too many cases in which a person has been denied parole due to this factor, which is cited in parole hearings as an official factor. This masking of what the parole seeks at a hearing only makes it a more unjust system, especially for those who have been wrongfully convicted and the only possible way to freedom is the admission to guilt and performing to an unrealistic problem. "Lifers, then, who go before the Parole Board and claim innocence need to support that claim with exculpatory evidence in order to overcome that there had been a trial, a conviction, an unsuccessful appeal, and the underlying presumption of guilt"." Even if the parole board and criminal justice system try to approach this matter of guilt and the power that comes with either imposing, accepting or denying it is present without a doubt.

On the other hand 116 (84.7%) of the cases were denied parole in 2013, a number that has been on the rise when it comes to parole hearing since 2009 when the first of these reports was made available by the group at MCI Norfolk. In 2009 the percentages of approvals and denials were 35 (38.9%) and 55 (61.1) but the number of hearings was also lower with 90 being the total for that year. It seems as less and less people are being seen as worth saving. Some factors for the denial of parole that feed into the need of repentance include; limited program participation, lying/not credible; diminishes responsibility, inconsistency between inmate's version and the facts of the case and last but not least lack of remorse.[21] The two sides of a parole hearing and the two possible outcomes are intrinsically very connected and the factors quite similar, with this the guideline on how to make the decision on who is worth saving and who is not rely solely on the parole board and how they interpret worthiness. There is much incongruence.

In one particular case of a person convicted to a life sentence, although a convicted person completed programs for the purpose of rehabilitation that would increase the chance for him to be granted parole. He is not granted parole based on the history and nature of the crime for which he or she has been convicted.[22] The offender brings up the fact that the crime for which he was convicted of was done under the influence of alcohol, and this is taken as a denial of culpability. With this case especially we see that although not officially stated as a requirement, the affirmation of being guilty of the crime in parole hearings is necessary to even begin to be considered as rehabilitated. From this it seems as if even if the person is innocent, there is no way to avoid confessing to the crime in order to continue the process and be deemed worthy of saving. Everyone before the parole board is presumed guilty of the convicted crime and denying means not being repentant and this approach only causes setbacks.

Sometimes the decision on whether to grant parole is made even before the hearing of the offender takes place. In the case of Vincent Simmons, subject of the HBO documentary THE FARM[23], Vincent having been convicted of rape maintains his innocence and heads to the hearing with evidence of this, but before he even gets a chance to speak for himself the victim offers a statement that yields a decision by the board. After the witness leaves, the parole board is heard expressing that there is really no need for the offender to even make a case because they have already made their decision based on the victims testimony rather than taking it into account as much Vincent's. Instead they ignore all the paperwork and medical proof that the victim was proven a virgin through medical tests, which took place after his arrest.[24]

Other times, although the convicted person explicitly communicates that they still struggle and are not completely rehabilitated, he or she gets approved for parole.[25] Incongruence in the way which decisions are made exists in the parole hearings. "There is no existing mechanism for presumptive parole in Massachusetts. As a result, all prisoners eligible for parole must go before the Parole Board, which can grant or deny parole based on the discretion of its members".[26] The parole board with various members cannot possibly have a singular representation of what rehabilitation is. But what is clear is that some of the common factors that are looked for when considering the granting of parole include; the demonstration of repentance, responsibility for actions, involvement in programs that help address the issues or reasons why the person landed in prison and the assurance that the convicted will not commit more offences.

Endnotes

1. The Shawshank Redemption (1994) - /MDb. (n.d.). Retrieved from http://www.imdb.com/title/tt0111161/
2. You Tube. "Morgan Freeman - The Shawshank Redemption -Montage rehabilitated prisoner - 40 years."
YouTube. https://www.youtube.com/watch?v=cG05rXUAH2o.
3. "Red's parole hearings in The Shawshank Redemption." - Movies & TV Stack Exchange. http://movies.stackexchange.com/questions/2022/reds-parole-hearings-in-the-shawshank-redemption.
4. "General Laws." :CHAPTER 127, Section 130. N.p., n.d. Web. 28 Apr. 2014.
<https://malegislature.gov/Laws/GeneralLaws/Partl/title/Chapter 127/Section130>.
5. "History." Public Safety and Security. http://www.mass.gov/eopss/law-enforce-and-cj/parole/paroleboard/history.html
6. Snyder, T. Richard. The Protestant ethic and the spirit of punishment. (Grand Rapids, Mich.: W.B. Eerdmans, 2001. Print.) 2
7. Parker, William. "The Origins of History of Parole." In "Parole": (origins, development, current practices, and statutes). (College Park, Md.: American Correctional Association, 1972)
8. Friedman, Lawrence Meir. Crime and punishment in American history. (New York: BasicBooks, 1993). e-book
9. Friedman, Crime and punishment in American history, e-book.
10. IBID
11. "USDOJ: U.S. Parole Commission: Frequently Asked Questions." USDOJ: U.S. Parole Commission: Frequently Asked Questions. http://www.justice.gov/uspc/faqs.html#q1 (accessed April 28, 2014).
12. "120 CMR: Parole Board." 120 Code of Massachusetts Regulations. http://www.lawlib.state.ma.us/source/mass/cmr/120cmr.html 300.04
13. "Decisions." Public Safety and Security. http://www.mass.gov/eopss/agencies/parole-board/lifer   cords-of-decision.html
14. Used a case of a lifer with possibility of parole hearing as an example of the elements that are taken into account at the time of a parole hearing. Prisons.org/materials/Haas-parole-decisions-for-lifers-2013-2014.pdf> 14"2014 Life Sentence Decisions."www.mass.gov. N.p., n.d. Web. 4 May 2014.
http://www.mass.gov/eopss/docs/pb/lifer.decisions/2014/williamsdavid3-5-14.pdf

15. Haas, Gordon, and Norfolk Lifers Group MCI Norfolk. "Materials." *PAROLE DECISION FOR LIFERS 2013-2014*. N.p., n.d. Web. 5 May 2014. 4 <http://www.realcostto

16. Haas, Gordon, and Norfolk Lifers Group MCI Norfolk, "Materials." *PAROLE DECISION FOR LIFERS 2013-2014*. 10

17. Ibid

18. "General Laws.": CHAPTER 127, Section 130. N.p., n.d. Web. 5 May 2014.
https://malegislature.gov/Laws/Generallaws/Partl!TitleXVI11/Chapter127/Section130>.

19. "2014 Life Sentence Decisions." (www.mass.gov. N.p., n.d. Web. 4 May 2014.) 11 <http:/fwww.mass.gov/eopssfdocsfpbflifer-decisions/2014fwilliamsqavid3-5-14 .Qdf>.

20. Haas, Gordon, and Norfolk Lifers Group MCI Norfolk. "Materials." (PAROLE DECISION FOR LIFERS 2013-2014. N.p., n.d. Web. 5 May 2014.) 13 <http://www.realcostofprisons.org/materials/Haas-parole decisions-for-lifers-2013-2014. pdf>.

21. Haas, Gordon, and Norfolk Lifers Group MCI Norfolk. "Materials." (PAROLE DECISION FOR LIFERS 2013-2014. N.p., n.d. Web. 5 May 2014.) 14 <http://www.realcostofprisons.org/materials/Haas-parole decisions-for-lifers-2013-2014. pdf>.

22. Used a case of a lifer with possibility of parole hearing as an example of the incongruence with the M.G.L. c. 127, § 130. This case can be found at: http://www.mass.gov/eopss/docs/pb/lifer decisions/2014/chavezgerson 1-30-14. pdf

23 IMDb.com. "The Farm: Angola, USA." IMDb. http://www.imdb.com/title/tt0139193/ (accessed April 28, 2014).

24. YouTube. "Shocking Parole Hearing of Vincent Simmons." YouTube. https://www.youtube.com/watch?v=4qerFurVN_A

25. Used a case of a lifer with possibility of parole hearing as an example of the incongruence with the M.G.L. c. 127, § 130. This case can be found at: http://www.mass.gov/eopss/docs/pb/lifer-decisions/2014/mongowarren2-4-14paroled.pdf

Works Cited

"120 CMR: Parole Board." 120 Code of Massachusetts Regulations.
    http://www.lawlib.state.ma.us/source/mass/crnr/l 20cmr.htrnl (accessed
    May 5, 2014).
"2014 Life Sentence
    Decisions."www.mass.gov.http://www.mass.gov/eopss/docs/pb/lifer
decisions/2014/williamsdavid3-5-14.pdf (accessed May 4, 2014).
"2014 Life Sentence Decisions.m
    "www.mass.gov.http://www.mass.gov/eopss/docs/pb/lifer
decisions/2014/williamsdavid3-5-14.pdf (accessed May 4, 2014).
"Decisions." Public Safety and Security.
    http://www.mass.gov/eopss/agencies/parole-board/lifer
records-of-decision.html (accessed May 5, 2014).
Friedman, Lawrence Meir. *Crime and punishment in American History*.
    New York: BasicBooks,
1993.
"General Laws.": CHAPTER 127, Section 130.
    https://malegislature.gov/Laws/GeneralLaws/PartI!fitleXVIII/Chapter
    127/Section l 30 (accessed May 5, 2014).
"General Laws." : CHAPTER 127, Section 130.
    https://malegislature.gov/Laws/GeneralLaws/PartI/TitleXVIII/Chapterl2
    7/Section130 (accessed May 5, 2014).
Haas, Gordon, and Norfolk Lifers Group MCI Norfolk. "Materials."
    PAROLE DECISION FOR LIFERS 2013-2014.
    http://www.realcostofprisons.org/materials/Haas-parole-decisions-for-
    lifers-
2013-2014 .pdf (accessed May 5, 2014).
"History." Public Safety and Security. http://ww.mass.gov/eopss/law-
    enforce-and
    cj/parole/parole-board/history.html (accessed May 5, 2014).
YouTube. "Morgan Freeman - The Shawshank Redemption -Montage
    rehabilitated prisoner - 40 years." YouTube.
    https://www.youtube.com/watch?v=cGo5rXUAH2o (accessed May 5,
    2014).
    Parker, William. "Parole": (origins, development, current practices, and
    statutes). College Park, Md.: American Correctional Association, 1972.
"Red's parole hearings in The Shawshank Redemption." - Movies & TV
    Stack Exchange. http://movies.stackexchange.com/questions/2022/reds-
    parole-hcarings-in-the-shawshank redemption (accessed May 5, 2014).

YouTube. "Shocking Parole Hearing of Vincent Simmons." YouTubc.
    htlps://www.youtube.com/watch?v=4qerFurVN_A (accessed May 5,
    2014).

Snyder, T. Richard. *The Protestant Ethic and the Spirit of Punishment.*
    Grand Rapids, Mich.: W.B. Eerdmans, 2001.

IMDb.com. "The Shawshank Redemption." IMDb.
    http://www.imdb.com/title/tt01 1 1 l61/ (accessed May 2, 2014).

"USDOJ: U.S. Parole Commission: Frequently Asked Questions." USDOJ:
    U.S. Parole Commission: Frequently Asked Questions.
    http://wvvw.justice.gov/uspc/faqs.html#q I (accessed May 5, 2014).

Boston Bar. "WHITE PAPER: THE CURRENT STATE OF PAROLE IN
    MASSACHUSETTS." CJPC.org. http.z/www.cjpc.org/Zu 1 3/White-
    Paper-Addendum-2.25.13 (accessed May 5, 2014).

Curating the Blues:
Prison-Radio Correspondence as an Act of Co-creation

Kye

"There's a riot goin on, down in cell block #9.

-Johnny Winter

"I know that into each life some rain, some hard times, is got to fall..."
-Etta James, "Drown in My Own Tears"

Imagine a Saturday night Blues and jazz program. The deejay shows up each week like clockwork, but there are fans who are even more dedicated -- those listening late at night from inside prisons. They cannot call in requests, but they can send letters.

This essay draws from an archive of letters, written over a five-year span, from men living in 8 different prisons in North Central Florida, to a radio show called "Nothin' But the Blues" (NBTB). Most letters to NBTB contained requests for songs, which sounds simple, but is not. A writer named Scott captures some of the complexity of the process:

The requests you play for me, it keeps us close to each others hearts and in each others thoughts as it does the rest of the family members that email requests ... My son is not much of a letter-writer but to know a 20-yr-old young man will take time out of his busy schedule of higher learning following in his fathers footsteps to become an electrical engineer, hacks out an email request to you for his dear old dad, my heart is filled with joy. [New River East Correctional Institution, 3/8/05]

This letter tells a story about who the letter-writer is. We learn about Scott's son, about his profession, and about his sense of pride in both. The letters are full of life, humor, stories, and sorrow. They discuss love, race, identity, hope, regret, and loneliness. The writers also often discuss how the radio show changed the way they "do their time." Participating in NBTB for these men was a nuanced process of storytelling, prioritizing, building and maintaining relationships, contextualizing, and offering opinions. Stuart Hall would call what they do a "negotiated reading" of the Blues, one which takes on some pieces of the dominant hegemonic position while rejecting other pieces and uncovering meanings more relevant to their situation. This essay seeks to uncover and articulate the range of meanings of a Saturday night Blues radio show for its fans who are incarcerated. I will argue that the men who wrote these letters, requesting songs, disputing claims, sharing life histories, and issuing darts and laurels, acted as co-curators of Nothin' But the Blues, creating a space of community and connection, both outside and within the walls of various prisons, writing letters that narrated stories of self and enacted agency in a way that ultimately disrupted the disciplining gaze of surveillance.

What it means to have the Blues

There is an American sense that punishment ought-to hurt, that it ought to make criminals "pay" (hence the descriptor "retributive," from Latin *retribuere*, to pay back). Snyder calls this impulse a "spirit of punishment," and argues that it holds the U.S. in its grip, causing us to separate ourselves physically and psychologically from those who are being punished. "Prisoners are frequently viewed as 'other," writes Snyder, "as if they were a different species."[1] In 1992, ten years before this archive of letters were written, Massachusetts governor William Weld held a press conference and voiced his belief that "prison should be like a tour through the circles of hell." This does seem to be what the writer-curators describe - almost all of them write about the "loneliness and darkness" of life in lockdown, in one form or another (Ari, New River East, 8/11/03). And there is a growing admission from authors like Michelle Alexander and Peter Moskos that retribution, once begun, doesn't end. As Alexander points out, it is "perfectly legal to discriminate against criminals."[2] so the punishment can go on indefinitely.

Given the sorrow that is bound to come from this deep, continued separation, who would not have "the Blues"? As the easy intelligibility of the phrase itself would suggest, culturally we understand the Blues as a medium that wears its sorrow on its sleeve, that contains a raw suffering, grappled with, eliciting powerful, meaningful public expression. The deepest expression of the Blues genre is a certain "gut-wrenching" beauty, as one writer-curator put it - played acoustically, the form is a sort of contemplation of pain, a 12-bar rumination on a theme with a twist at the end.[3] When Blues goes electric, it can become a wailing expression of pain put to music.[4] "Blues" seems (to those imprisoned and those who are not) a perfectly appropriate accompaniment to "punishment."

Stuart Hall would call this a hegemonic decoding of the Blues - a decoding of the message of Blues that fits comfortably within a dominant social framework. Those being punished by the broader society should suffer, and it is therefore appropriate that they listen to music suffused with pain and suffering. However, Hall's theory of decoding allows for readings of cultural products that are "negotiated," readings that acknowledge the dominant meanings but finding new meanings according to "local conditions," using "situated logics."[5] Pop culture theorist Carla Freccero seems to refer to this practice of the negotiated reading with her use of the phrase "subculture." Freccero defines subculture as "groups within the dominant or hegemonic culture that express a relation of resistance, opposition, or refusal to the larger culture."[6]

The writer-curators of NBTB - as members of this 'subculture' - expressed resistance, opposition, and refusal to the prison system through their letters and curating activities. We see an example of the complexity in a letter from Pablo, at United States Penitentiary, in Coleman, Florida: "I'm a Texas-Mexican that got the Blues over here in this New U.S. Pen in Coleman. Just joking - if you can't do the time, don't do the crime .. ." He is acknowledging his sorrow (with a hegemonic reading of "the Blues" that is well-established in American popular parlance), then disallowing himself the latitude to feel sorrow (using a widely-known phrase of retribution, 'if you can't do the time, don't do the crime,' to remind himself that he is guilty and he must hone his skills at 'doing time so it does not destroy him).

But the rest of Pablo's letter (which will be featured later in more detail) undoes both of those initial hegemonic readings-- he may have the Blues, and he may need to suck it up, but he also is able to recount memories of Blues fandom, articulate a deeply felt appreciation of two female Blues musicians, and fire the opening salvo in a conversation about which one is a better Blues musician. Though his engagement as a curator is placed with statements that imply both that he is suffering and that he deserves no sympathy, his stories and opinions seem to have a healing and entertaining function, as well as a certain curatorial credential-building function. Blues is a genre with a history of underground messages--the Blues often sheaths joy or humor in its sorrow. Likewise, referencing "the Blues" in this collection of letters did often contain a certain culturally imposed heaviness, the re-establishment of the writer-curator as a person in prison, but this sorrow was often interwoven in the letters with the lightness and enthusiasm of fandom, and the self-assurance of expertise.

The Unbearable Indelibility of Being in Prison

That heaviness of punishment is not easy to overcome. Prison creates a character, the "delinquent," Foucault tells us, a subject who is abnormal, hardened -- in popular imagination, likely a member of a lower social class. Benedict Anderson pioneered the notion of the imagined community, the understanding we have of who "we" are, even if we'll never meet all the members of the community we imagine to be like us. The delinquent, in the popular imagination, is not "one of us." Foucault imagines "[t]he establishment of a delinquency that constitutes something like an enclosed illegality" --people in prison must be entirely illegal in order that people and institutions outside of prison can be understood to be "legal." Too, people in prison must also be entirely illegal because they are entirely incarcerated, not partially.[7] Quickly, with the penitentiary system, we see "the fabrication of a delinquency that [the prison system] is supposed to combat."[8]

As opposed to public punishments like flogging, Foucault argues that the point of the penitentiary is ongoing surveillance. It is documentation of movement,[9] "knowledge of each inmate, of his behaviour, his deeper states of mind, his gradual improvement. .. places of clinical knowledge ... under permanent observation; every report that can be made about him must be recorded and computed."[10] Foucault points to the innovative prison designs of Jeremy Bentham, who came up with the Panopticon, the central guard tower with visual access to every part of the prison. Bentham described it thus: "a new mode of obtaining power of mind over mind."[11]

Foucault describes the essence of the Panopticon as a gaze that may or may not be present, but which always *could* be present: "The inmate must never know whether he is being looked at at any one moment but he must be sure that he may always be so."[12] It is an intimacy and tight control that is a different bodily invasion than outright violence, but it *is* an invasion, one which is ongoing and thorough. Foucault writes, "The theme of the Panopticon -- at once surveillance and observation, security and knowledge, individualization and totalization, isolation and transparency ... making it possible to substitute for force or other violent constraints the gentle efficiency of total surveillance .. ."[13] Surveillance, as Foucault describes, contains its own horrors. This, both the indelible mark of "delinquent" and its isolation, its shame and its total exposure, are part of what is resisted, if not escaped, I will argue, through these letters of engagement with Blues radio.

Kathy Halbreich is an innovative curator now with the Museum of Modern Art in New York. She is known for re-thinking the role of the museum to participate in the community that surrounds it, for working to make art more accessible and more relevant to the life of its community. This also involved re-thinking the nature of community itself. When she worked in Milwaukee, WI, at the Walker Art Center, that institution was among the first to decide that setting up online exhibits could change the number of people

Experiencing the art they had to offer, as well as creating a new, online community that did not depend on shared brick-and-mortar space to come together. While other curators talk about a museum director or curators as "the brain within the museum."[14] Halbreich considers the creation, appreciation, and discussion a community process. Judith Rugg, an artist and art-theorist, describes a "web of co-dependent authors" that arises when a specific site hosts an art installation.[15] It was similar with NBTB. Pratt defines "contact zones" as "social spaces where cultures meet, clash, grapple with each other, often in highly asymmetrical relations of power."[16] Prison is a contact zone. NBTB, too, is a contact zone, but one in which all engage by writing letters, and all voices that engage are heard and responded to. NBTB was a space where people, curators and artists, could connect, and form their own imagined community.

Making Requests

One way of naming membership in a community, imagined or otherwise, is by making a request of that community. Writing in a request seems a simple enough process. We have our favorites; we want to hear them because it makes us happy.[17] But is a song just a song, or a request just a request? In fact, much is contained in these song requests, and examining some of their complexity helps put us on the road to seeing the act of co-curating that takes place by listeners who are incarcerated.

What exactly is happening when Pablo writes to request: "I'd rather go blind," sung by Koko Taylor, to the guys in USP Coleman? It is a song about the pain of losing love,[18] that was made popular in the 1960s by Etta James. But too it is a move designed to build community, resist the controls that say a prisoner cannot communicate with others after lights-out, to remember a particular time in history, and to make life a little more interesting for himself and others. Benedict Anderson writes that people who identify as part of a large community "will never know many of their fellow members, meet them ... yet in the minds of each lives the image of their communion."

"Though all the men in a prison might not know one another, they may create what Anderson calls "imagined community."[19] Frequently media works to create that sense of community -- media that people in prison aren't normally able to access. Pablo is helping to create a sense of affinity. What's so subversive about that? To answer that question, we only need return to the history of the penitentiary system in the U.S.

Moskos and other authors trace the historical importance of isolation in the U.S. penitentiary system. In Eastern State Penitentiary, the first penitentiary, the planners (heavily influenced by Bentham of Panopticon fame) decided to install individual toilets, at a time when not even the President of the United States enjoyed indoor plumbing, rather than allowing a communal bathroom."[20] Moskos writes, "The goal, prison commissioners said, was to keep prisoners so isolated that if they were in prison on election night, they wouldn't know who was president of the United States when they were released."[21] If the essence of punishment is control and isolation, fellow-feeling and good-faith efforts to build a sense of community undermine the totality of punishment.

In that spirit, bearing in mind the common stories of people who have driven a long way to visit prisoners and been turned away for wearing the wrong clothing, or who have been kept waiting for hours and watched the time they would get to spend with their loved one dwindle to a pittance, it is important to underline the importance of radio requests coming from lovers and family members of those incarcerated. Emails and letters from family members and lovers of those who were "on the inside" provided a different way of maintaining contact, when visits might have been scarce, uncertain, or closely controlled. It offered lovers a way to be together on Saturday night, and let their thoughts run wild. The requests, too, contain the hope of continuing connection, though loved ones are living with separation. As Scott said about the request from his son, "it keeps us close to each others hearts and in each others thoughts." (New River, 3/8/05).

Yet another way requests were used was to offer well-wishes and encouragement for other inmates. For example, a request came in for James Sand, AKA "The Sand Man." A friend he'd met inside, Kevin, wrote:

[James] is a 26-year-old white guy from Chicago. For the last year and a half he's been learning how to play the guitar. He's even written a few Blues songs. His goal is to take his craft to the next level when he gets out of here in 3 more years. And I think he has what it takes to make that dream come true. I also believe that it would help his cause if he could get a little encouragement from someone special. That's where you come in. All I want you to do is say something like you heard that he's pretty good at what he does and that if he keeps workin' at it, his dreams will soon be attainable." (Lake Butler, 7/21/03)

This human act of kindness and encouragement flies in the face of all that is labeled "delinquent" about Kevin or about James. As Thomas Merton wrote, by loving others, we make them worthy of our love, and we are made worthy ourselves by the act of loving. In another letter, a man named Jeff requested the band WAR, singing "Whose Cadillac is That" (such a catchy, on-top-of-the-world tune about driving cars and sunny days) and dedicated it "for my roommate Tom." These kind gestures reveal Blues radio as a safe space for men to express care for one another, to resist a prison masculinity that required dominance over caring impulses.

Transcending "Time"

In prisons, Taylor writes, "time is turned into a weapon of terror. It can also be wielded by authorities-lengthened, shaped by routine-and thus is an important aspect of the criminal justice system's theatrics of terror... The routinization of time is a transformation cultivated by prison authorities and designed to make every day like every other."[22] Taylor cites Mumia Abu-Jamal's thoughts on the subject of boredom and the passage of time. Abu-Jamal has spent the last 30 years of his life in prison: "The mind-numbing, soul-killing savage sameness that makes each day an echo of the day before, with neither thought nor hope of growth."[23] Abu-Jamal calls this "Spirit death." Listening to the first two bars of Etta James' "Love and Happiness," we may know what it is to be transported, swept away by a song - to be utterly saved from a death of the spirit. This was another function of Nothin' But the Blues for its listeners/writers/curators.

Writer-curators frequently mentioned that listening to Blues radio brought a different, sometimes even transcendent, experience of space and time to their Saturday night. Being able to lose oneself in the moment and forget time, or being mentally transported by music to a state of joy or to a place of memory- this itself, in a prison, is a form of escape."[NBTB] is the only quantum leap (escape) I have to free myself of this horrid place," writes Scott (New River East, 5/30/04). Dwight, a man with 8 months until his release, wrote: "I'm always looking forward for your next show on Saturday nights. Because it gives me something I like and enjoy so much So it truly helps me do my time better... your Blues show is very precious to me." (Union Correctional, 06/02/05) Having something you like, something to look forward to, in prison, is precious indeed.

A listener named Eddie had been in prison in Indiana before Florida, and had relied on a steady string of radio shows throughout his time in prison. The radio programs had accompanied him, made his time more bearable, and allowed him to function without allowing his spirit to die: "I'll be going home in 2007, work release ... I've made it through because of people who do radio programs like yours ... Indiana State U has a radio show that does Blues on two nights of the week, and these two guys kept me rock in'. If it weren't for ISU, and this radio station called "The River" 105.5 that plays Classic Rock. I would have went nuts up there in Terre Haute Federal Prison." (Coleman, 05/04/04)

Ari, a college kid about a year into a 2 year sentence for selling ecstasy, wrote:

> As usual, I caught last week's show ... That Jimi Hendrix made me feel like I was back home in a bubble-filled bathtub with a tall drink in my hand and nothin' to do but live on the edge of each one of those thick, earthy notes until I almost died ... or until the water got cold, whichever came first. LOL. That's what I have missed the most: Baths. I'm not queer or anything, but there is a special something to be said for the old tradition of just relaxing by candlelight and soaking your stress away to some deep, Southern-fried Blues. Nothin' but existing ... [peace sign]

Listening to Jimi Hendrix transported him, in his mind, into a hot bath.

Donald wrote that he was in pain, as he'd slipped in a water puddle earlier in the year, and couldn't seem to get any relief.

> There's a song I don't know who sings it but my parents used to sing it whenever my other 6 siblings or myself was sick. Kiddy 0. It starts off, 'I wrote you a 6-page letter, I even called you on the telephone, I can't stand this waste of pick me up, don't let me down. I want you say yes and don't say no, it makes me feel good, kiddy-o.' (09/10/04)

Donald was invoking a time of comfort, marshalling his emotional resources to try to feel better.

Though I couldn't find the track at the time in our library,[24] perhaps in writing out those words Donald was able to sing that song to himself, in an act of self-soothing. In the same letter, he also requested Sam Cooke, "A Change is Gonna Come," so it seems likely that I played him that song instead. Sending Donald out well-wishes for his health seems like the key. Even if he didn't get just what he wanted, he got wishes for his health from someone on the outside. Whether or not he got the outcome he asked for, he was still using his voice, adding his Jamaican-inflected notion of Blues to the conversation.

All of the writer-curators in this section are calling upon other parts of their lives, places where they survived or felt joy and comfort, to sustain them. They are drawing on inner resources, and Blues act as a vehicle for that. This act of Curating Blues in prison means not just curating a show, but curating the self-- resisting the power of the prison mechanism to define and control how they see themselves, actively choosing and emphasizing certain stories, culling them for meaning, writing narratives, narrating proficiencies and skills that generate a competent sense of self.

The act of Story-telling

This act of curating the self is also seen clearly when writer-curators choose to do story-telling in their letters. Ari, the college student, concerned that prison would make its mark, began a letter in June of 2003 with these words: "A man who has been in another world does not come back unchanged. One can't put the difference into words...Little things in his conversation, little mannerisms, accidental allusions which he made and then drew back with an awkward apology, all suggested that he had been keeping strange company." These words came from C.S. Lewis' book

Perelandra. "That was one of my major fears coming into the Florida prison system," Ari wrote, "that I would be 'changed ...' Anyway, God has been good to me in my sojourn through the wilderness. I have met a lot of different personalities to use for character reference and dialect in my future writing, so it hasn't been a total loss. I always try to see the good in any situation; an eternal optimist. But to say that I have not been affected at all by this psychologically depressive and degrading system of humiliation would be a mistake. I will say this: Never again in my life will I choose to judge another upon any premise other than how they treat or regard others." Ari also sent lyrics to songs he was working on, and a constant stream of adulation for Jimi Hendrix, including the rare tracks with the phone ringing in the background. If by day Ari was told to conform and submit to control, that his personhood didn't matter as much as his obedience, with the Blues show as an outlet, he could pursue a hobby, gush over his favorite musician, process his prison experience in writing, and engage in some self-building by declaring himself an "eternal optimist" and describing the ways that prison would help him in the future. (New River East, 6/24/03).

This optimism was fairly common in letters to NBTB, despite the hegemonic view of Blues as a sad and sorrowful genre. In June of 2005, Dwight wrote, "It won't be long until I go to Blues jams again. Only 8 months to go! Then back to Pensacola." He is invoking the future, sharing his story and keeping his spirits up. Several prison bands wrote with some regularity, and the Brickyard Blues Band of the Federal Corrections Complex in Coleman, Florida, even sent a photo and stories of their shows. Their front man, Darryl, or "Hollywood Slim," wrote that they were trying to get recorded when they all got out.

Writer-curator Eddie wrote a glowing vision of the future, literally riding off into the sunset: "I'm from South Florida, Ft. Lauderdale to be exact. .. Hey, girl, if you're ever cruising through Davie,[25] and see a light-skinned black male on a horse, that most likely will be me. I'm a cowboy at heart and I love cowgirls with a passion ... By the way Howlin' Wolf is my most favorite Blues man, and Big Mama Thornton is my Bluesgirl." (Coleman, 04/05/04) Blues is a genre that turns on a discussion of race, appropriation, and racialized experience. Writing letters to a Blues program allowed the discussion of race, while building multi-racial community or subculture inside a prison system where relating across race lines can be complicated. This topic ought to be explored in another essay.

Co-curating the Blues

The Blues genre, and this co-curating, too, must be examined as a "contact zone," which Pratt calls [a] "social space where cultures meet, clash, grapple with each other, often in highly asymmetrical relations of power."[26] White, brown and black, inside the walls and outside the walls, college-educated and educated in the school of hard knocks - these cultures were coming together to claim meaning around Blues music. The Blues fans in prison offered mentorship to me as a deejay and student of the Blues, while at the same time they were taught new songs, new versions of songs, and bands by listening to the show. It was a learning community.

Writer-curators reveal their curatorial aesthetic easily. For Greg (Sumter Correctional Institution, 6/8/03) knowing a song or lick's genealogy is key, as is understanding the way a song has traveled, which reveals in his mind which musicians are original and which are derivative. He requests Pat Travers' version of "Boom, Boom (Out Go the Lights),"[27] saying that Travers "doesn't get enough credit," but identifies the song as belonging to Little Walter. "I'm a Blues guitar player," Greg discloses, and goes on to list a group of guitarists, both black and white, some of whom play acoustic country Blues and others electric urban Blues. He includes Lightning Hopkins. "(Beck rips him off)," he writes. He has little patience for the mainstream appropriation of Blues: "I thought you might like to know George Harrison and the Beatles did a Blues song ... I mean 'For yer Blues.' George even says 'Elmore James got nothing on this baby.' Well maybe George should have stuck to his Carl Perkins licks as on 'Everybody's trying to be my baby.'" In trying to say he could best Elmore James, in Greg's eyes, George Harrison is out of his depth -- he'd better step back into shallower water with the simple rock-Blues riffs of white country Blues artist Carl Perkins.

Jeff "the Juiceman" (Union Correctional Institution, 08/05/05) requested all white plugged-in Blues musicians from Detroit and New York, but "Whiskey-Drinkin' Woman" by Nazareth he identified as "Blues-ish." He was choosing the things he enjoyed most, but he was also engaged in the project of curating genre, in drawing lines between straight Blues and Blues-rock fusion. Ari, the college student, voiced dissatisfaction with the show's timeslot, which decreased for some months from 3 hours each Saturday night to 2 hours. The men had been accustomed to 3 hours of music each Saturday night, 11pm-2am, but a programming shift put an indie rock show in the 1a-2am slot. "It sucks that your show has been trimmed down to 2 hours," Ari wrote (NRE, 5/22/03). Several men wrote about that late-night issue, asking if it could play earlier in the evening because they had to get up for work in the morning, or because they had trouble staying awake for it. Particularly given the time controls present for people living in prison, this seems an important curatorial move, an important muscle to keep using. As when hanging an art show, it can be a challenge to that presence of mind, that ability to step back, look critically and say, "This does not work for me, can we move it?"

Returning to Pablo at USP Coleman, his letter is notable in terms of its curatorial agenda. "Got a beef with you, Blues Girl, How can you say that Etta James is 'the Queen of the Blues.' Koko Taylor is the only QOTB." He is correct, in fact! Koko Taylor is the undisputed Queen of the Blues,[28] Etta James is known as the *Matriarch* of the Blues. Pablo wants me to know there are no hard feelings: "Etta James," he says, "I dig that light-skin sister. I'm from Texas but raised in Los Angeles, back in the 60s when she used to jam in L.A. Went to a few of her jam-sessions." But Pablo's request, "I'd rather go blind"[29] (sung by Koko Taylor, to the guys in USP Coleman) takes on new meaning. It is a curatorial decision, asking for a signature Etta James song (recorded 1967, Muscle Shoals) performed by Koko Taylor. If we look at the context of the conversation, Pablo was asking me to listen more deeply to Koko, to understand why she had this position of deep respect, so I would not mix up those titles in the future.

Niolasc Serota is the director of the Tate museums. At a conference of curators in Philadelphia in 2000, he said that curating "Art is not simply a matter of like or dislike, it's a matter of responding to a whole set of experiences put together by another individual or group of individuals and responding to that. The curator has to try and mediate this work in a manner that reveals knowledge but does not intimidate."[30] Pablo did that. He subtly asked for a song that would show me what he already knew about Koko Taylor. And it is an incredible song. She does a beautiful job with "I'd Rather Go Blind."[31] This is not to say that I changed my mind! Etta is still a bit closer to my heart than Koko. Yes, she's got pop, jazz and R & B inflections, she's not a straight-up blues performer like Koko. Yes, she even sang with Steve Winwood. But there's something really powerful to me in Etta's subtlety, where Koko really shouts the blues. The point is not that we agree, but maybe that I'll never forget who the undisputed Queen of the Blues is, and that I tried on the glasses from Pablo's point of view, which is what Halbreich and Rugg are pointing to, the power in a community, a web, of creators and curators. Particularly in the Blues community, a dedicated group with an emotional stake, each person has a stake in how the Blues are presented and preserved.

Feeding the Spirit

Curating had life-giving properties for the men writing into the show, truly it seemed to fight the "death of the Spirit." It was not merely a way of creating a sense of personhood through exercising expertise, it was a way of renewing and honoring life. "One man, Scott, the one whose son sent in a request, also received dedications from his mother and other relatives. But for him the curatorial act was a way of showing love to other inmates, a way of setting aside his own concerns to put others first. Right before Christmas in 2004, for instance, he made a few special requests. He wrote back the very next week:

> Thank you so much for playing the request I asked for in my last letter. If you could only have seen the joy on the faces of Drew, Chris and Mr Bloodsworth. Wow. Drew & Chris are in my dorm and when the requests were played I went over to their bunks and seen the joyful tears streaming down their cheeks. It was wonderful. Andy and I have family to send mail to us, receive calls and send song requests for us. The others have nothing and were so overwhelmed to know someone out there had sent a request in for them alone. They just couldn't believe it. Mr. Bloodworth is in another dorm so I couldn't see his reaction but Sunday he came to me where I work in the Law Library. He rushed up to the counter saying, 'Did you hear, did you hear, someone out there played a song request for me.' He said, 'Who could it have been?' He's such a sweet old man. It felt great to see such joy in his smile that day. He asked me if I knew anything about the request or who it could have been from and I said, 'Mr Bloodworth I guess there really is a Santa Claus out there somewhere, huh.' I think he knew but said nothing as I noticed right then his eyes swelled up and in the corner, one single tear spilled out and trickled

down the side of his face. I've never seen that man cry or show any sign of weakness but this touched his heart. Thank you. (12/19/04)

That Christmas, Scott engaged in building community, in an act of accompaniment and friendship, in cementing the bonds of this group of friends. This was a place to show affection that was outside the system, that was secret and silent and intimate enough to allow some of these men the space to cry with joy at being remembered at Christmas.

Cur(at)ing the 'delinquent'

Snyder writes that, in the U.S., when it comes to crime, "we'd rather turn the knife than turn the other cheek."[32] Eating, sleeping, responding to control, all these things are done by animals. Developing a skill, honing an aesthetic, expressing a deeply held belief, and doing meta-level thinking on how things are to be classified and what makes one thing more or less real than another ... that is a clear expression of humanity. Those are not the actions of a "delinquent." They are the actions of a human being. So much more so, choosing to care for another who is in pain, fearing for your own soul when it is caged, and looking for ways to care for your soul and express your feelings about it. These ways of being human in prison become survival techniques, and modes of resistance.

Jesse Krimes had been a high-level drug dealer, but became an artist in prison, using bed sheets as canvas, colored pencils, and hair gel to transfer newspaper images to the fabric, which he would then color and manipulate. He created a 39-panel mural that he sent piece by piece to his family. When he got out, he finally could see all the pieces together. As one author observed, "The laborious routine kept Krimes sane, focused and disciplined." And Krimes himself writes, "Doing this was a way to fight back, the system is designed to make you into a criminal and make you conform. I beat the system?"[33]

NBTB could not be counted upon as a certainty, though it could be a space of reprieve and community. It was possible to be denied the chance to engage. As one listener/curator explained, you could lose radio privileges, or run out of batteries before Saturday night, you could fall asleep, there could be an electrical storm and you could lose reception, your letter might not arrive, or the deejay might not play your song. And the panopticon was never entirely absent. Though the men could create or honor any part of their story in a letter, that letter could still be read by a prison officer. Also, the men's lives were available to surveillance of a sort at any hour of the day or night on the Florida state inmate lookup web site, which posts sentences, crimes, personal information and photos of all incarcerated people in the state.

Still, this community of Blues enthusiasts and co-curators reaches toward Snyder's understanding of "the social nature of sin and redemption."[34] We do not sin in isolation, nor should we suffer in isolation. Understanding the uses of a weekly Blues radio show for Blues fans in prison struggling to hold onto their humanity honors the building of community that took place in that site, the messages that were passed there, beyond the approval of the wardens, the acts of critique and curating that these men took part in, and the emotions expressed, which included sorrow, dissatisfaction, curiosity, excitement and lust.

The writer-curators found many uses for NBTB -- it was a vehicle for story-telling and expertise, a place to connect to family, a place to decide what constituted blues and to increase their learning and community, a place to love and encourage other men in prison. Each of these uses served to resist inappropriate control, build community, and address boredom. Prison exerts control over self-image, over recreation, over how one uses one's time, over contact with loved ones and friends. Boredom is used as a weapon in prison to control and subdue, and is one of the hardest parts of "doing time."[35] Moskos calls prison "a total institution of complete dominance and regulation."[36] Engagement with NBTB undermined that complete dominance and regulation, in allowing spaces that were under the radar for communication and community building. When people in prison engaged with NBTB, this allowed (in keeping with Snyder's understanding that "sin is a corporate, collective reality... so too is redemption"[37]) for communal processing of grief, of joy, of regret, of hopes for the future, and community, inside and outside the walls of prisons.

Endnotes

1   Snyder, Protestant Ethic, ix.
2   Alexander, New Jim Crow, 2.
3   We hear this in many acoustic tunes. One interesting recorded example is Jimi Hendrix' "Hear My Train a-Comin'." https://www.youtube.com/watch?v==HrhsBYhfgEo
4   Stevie Ray Vaughan's electric "Tin Pan Alley" is wildly dynamic, it both contemplates and wails. This version was recorded live in Japan in 1985: https://www.youtube.com/watch?v==85v4T-Q51io
5   Hall, "Encoding/Decoding," 515. According to Hall's model, there may also be an oppositional reading, a decoding done against the grain, in which entirely new meanings are created. I have not found a truly oppositional decoding of Blues present in this group of letters, as the Blues are very rarely understood outside of a context of suffering. I believe that the possibility of experiencing both deep enjoyment and deep sorrow within the limits of a single genre helps to illuminate why it resonated so clearly with this group. Thinking about the complex emotional palette of the Blues could constitute another paper.
7   This idea sounds outlandish because we are so accustomed to this system, but many in-between states could exist, both for bodies and for. Imagine a person who is in prison during the day and goes home to sleep at night. Or imagine Bernie Madoff on house arrest.
8   Foucault, Discipline, 278.
9   ibid., 250.
10   Foucault, Discipline, 249.
11   Moskos, Flogging, 32.
12   Foucault, Discipline, 201.
13   I bid., 249.
14   Curating Now, 84.
15   Rugg & Sedgwick, Issues in Curating, 10.
16   Pratt, "Arts of the Contact Zone," 24.
17   An example: I love Otis Rush's "Hungry Country Girl." The song's main theme is that his woman will not leave him because he feeds her too well. It has many great lines, including: "And she better not ACT like she hungry, else a cow... dead." https://www.youtube.com/watch?v=26AllW7w9k4
18   Something deep down in my soul said, 'Cry, girl'/ When I saw you and that girl walkin' out/ I would rather, I would rather go blind, boy/ Than to see you walk away from me...
19   Anderson, Imagined Community, 15.
20   Moskos, Flogging, 40.

21 ibid.

22 Taylor, Executed God, 22.

23 ibid.

24 I've since discovered it on YouTube - it was old reggae, which definitely had a Blues feel to it, and would have fit into the show really well, in fact, so his curating was impeccable. https://www.youtube.com/watch?v=KqcjNPBiy24

25 Davie is an area of Florida with lots of horses-there is a horse hitch outside the Wendy's drive-through.

26 Pratt, "Arts," 34.

27 This song threatens physical violence toward a woman who has decided to leave a relationship with the person singing: "I never been so mad before/ when I found out she ain't mine no more. If I get her in my sight/ Boom, boom! Out go the lights."

28 She even has an album, Royal Blue (Alligator, 2000), that points to this fact.

29 "Something deep down in my soul said, 'Cry, girl'/ When I saw you and that girl walkin' out/ I would rather, I would rather go blind, boy/ Than to see you walk away from me...

30 Curating Now, 85.

31 Koko Taylor singing "I'd Rather Go Blind" https://www.youtube.com/watch?v=Hpvm4GbnFZQ

32 Snyder, Protestant Ethic, 1.

34 Snyder, 69.

35 Taylor, Executed God, 22. Moskos quotes a prisoner on an online message board: "At the end of the day it's the fucking boredom." Moskos, Flogging, 55.

36 Moskos, Flogging, 5.

37 ibid.' 66.

Sources

Alexander, Michelle. 2010. *The new Jim Crow: mass incarceration in the age of colorblindness.* New York: New Press.

Anderson, Benedict R. O'G. 1991. *Imagined communities: reflections on the origin and spread of nationalism.* London: Verso.

Casal-Data, Victoria, "Prisoner Creates Epic Mural OuOf Bedsheets, Hair Gel, And Newspapers As a Meditation On Heaven, Hell, And Redemption," March 10, 2014. Last accessed May 2, 2014.

http://beautifuldecay.com/2014/03/10/prisoner-creates-epic-mural-bedsheets-hair-gel-newspapers-meditation-heaven-hell-redemption/

Foucault, Michel. 1977. *Discipline and punish: the birth of the prison.* New York: Pantheon Books.

Freccero, Carla. 1999. *Popular culture an introduction.* New York: New York University Press.

Friedman, Lawrence M. 1993. *Crime and punishment in American history.* New York: BasicBooks.

Hall, Stuart "Encoding/Decoding," *Critical Visions In Film Theory.* Ed. Timothy Corrigan, P. White, M. Mazaj. Boston: Bedford St. Martins 2011. 77-87.

Marincola, Paula, and Robert Storr. 2001. *Curating now: imaginativepractice, public responsibility.* Philadelphia, PA: Philadelphia Exhibitions Initiative

Moskos, Peter. 2011. *In defense of flogging.* New York: Basic Books.

Rugg, Judith, and Michele Sedgwick. 2007. *Issues in curating contemporary art and performance.* Bristol, UK: Intellect.

Snyder, T. Richard. 2001. *The Protestant ethic and the spirit of punishment.* Grand Rapids, Mich: W.B. Eerdmans.

Taylor, Mark L. 2001. *The executed God: the way of the cross in lockdown America.*Minneapolis, Minn: Fortress Press.

Prisons and Playacting: Reclaiming Agency and Identity Through the Prison Arts Project at MECC

Adam Vander Tuig

"It was more horrible than I thought," admits Jack Hitt.[1]

"One guy I particularly liked shot a man in the head twice at point blank range. Another of my new friends raped his pubescent daughter, impregnating her. Later there was an abortion. Another friend grabbed a man getting out of a car, put a gun to his chest during a robbery and pulled the trigger. Others had sodomized children, younger children, the age of my own children."[2]

Later that night—after a full day of reading through files in a records depository in downtown St. Louis, and finally alone in bed in his hotel room—Hitt suffered multiple violent nightmares. In one, at a dear friend's home for an evening dinner party, and with several other guests present, Hitt's close friend begins to quarrel with a dinner guest, and, as the confrontation escalates, she pulls a gun and fires into the guest's face twice. Afterward, the friend, a fellow reporter, requests that Hitt keep the incident between the two of them.

"And the next thing I knew I was sitting up in my hotel bed, panting like a sprinter," he recounts. "It didn't take Freud to figure out what it meant. Someone I knew and liked was a murderer. I wanted to talk to the cast about this, but I was anxious. I know this sounds crazy, but I was afraid I might hurt their feelings. I felt like they had betrayed me. But strangely, I felt that I had betrayed them, too."[3]

The all-male cast to which Hitt refers—which included a number of men whom he came to know and like, and only one of whom who had any previous acting experience—was unique. Equally unique was the production of Shakespeare's *Hamlet* in which these men participated, their performance taking place over three years. It was produced and performed only within the prison walls of the institution in which all these men, except Hitt, were incarcerated: the Missouri Eastern Correctional Center (MECC) in Pacific, MO.

In 2002, reporter Jack Hitt spent several months visiting the MECC to cover director Agnes Wilcox, the actors, and the last two installments of their production of *Hamlet* as part of the Prison Arts Project, a program that brings arts and culture opportunities into jails, prisons, and detention and correctional centers. "Because it's against the rules to congregate an audience of felons for the four hours it would take to perform the whole play," explains Hitt, Wilcox had no other choice than to stage one act every six months from 1999 to the final, fifth act in 2002.[4] Hitt's coverage became the material for an entire hour-long episode of *This American Life*, entitled "Act V," which was broadcast in August of 2002.

The goal of this written exercise is to draw from Hitt's report to answer the following thesis question: how does the experience of the men involved in this production—as narrated by Hitt, and described by Wilcox and the men themselves—illustrate the ways in which this prison arts program was able to cultivate and restore a multiplicity of personal, individual agencies—the capacities one has for acting independently and autonomously, according to their own free will—for the men who are, or were incarcerated at MECC? In laying groundwork for answering this question, this paper also draws from many of the texts we read and discussed together in class. It is organized by a review of the ways in which people identified as criminals or offenders in America have been subject to public and private—often violent—denial of individual agency, and a history of the structural systems which have perpetuated this denial, then by an extended analysis of the ways in which playacting cultivates and restores agency to the men participating in the MECC production of *Hamlet*, and, finally, by a concluding discussion of how prison art programs like the one at MECC contribute constructively to a larger shift in cultural attitudes regarding people who are incarcerated in correction facilities in this country.

Two notes of clarification before I proceed, however: the first is that the text which I cite in this paper comes from the transcript of the aforementioned This American Life episode, but that for maximum effect, the fifty-nine-minute broadcast—which is available free online—deserves its own listen. The website itself provides the following note as preface to the transcript from which I take my text:

Note: *This American Life* is produced for the ear and designed to be heard, not read. We strongly encourage you to listen to the audio, which includes emotion and emphasis that's not on the page. Transcripts are generated using a combination of speech recognition software and human transcribers, and may contain errors. Please check the corresponding audio before quoting in print.[5]

The second note of clarification identifies where I stand as author of this paper. I write here as a former fine and performing arts major (literature and instrumental music) and as a former fine and performing arts educator as well. In addition, while I make only little mention of the spiritual and religious agency, which, as we will see, theater arts participation can cultivate and restore, it is also true that I write as a seminary student and future minister. That noted, let us now turn to a short history of punishment in America.

In Lawrence M. Friedman's *Crime and Punishment in American History*, Friedman writes the following in his introduction: "Criminal justice is a kind of social drama, a living theater; all of us are the audience; we learn morals and morality, right from wrong, wrong from right, through watching, hearing, and absorbing."[6] Friedman's use of the language of drama and theater arts is appropriate, and helps characterize much of the way America has pursued the punishment of offenders and criminals since its earliest colonial days. Trials in New Haven Colony, for example, were indeed "a kind of divine social theater," he writes.[7]

In these early dramas "theatrical elements came out with special force at hangings," and the "condemned were expected to play the role of the penitent sinner; it was best of all if they offered a final confession, a prayer, and affirmed their faith, in the very shadow of the gallows."[8] For the condemned—whether guilty or not—an established script existed, and was expected to be followed, effectively forsaking any real political agency on their part. That is, for the condemned, the only dramatic role available was that of the repentant sinner. The aim, after all, "was not just to punish, but to teach a lesson, so that the sinful sheep would want to get back to the flock. Punishment tended to be exceedingly public. The magistrates loved confessions of guilt, open expressions of remorse. They loved to enlist the community, the bystanders; their scorn, and the sinners' humiliation." Only a single dramatic role available to the condemned, it was also a role that was to be performed on a public stage. In some cases, the condemned person was forced to play the part in perpetuity: "Branding and letter-wearing were ways of marking an offender publicly—like sitting in the stocks, but far more permanently. The messages was that *this* offender was not likely to mend his ways; disgrace would and should last until death."[10] Only one part to be played, and for these unfortunate souls, it was to be played unto death.

It was not until the nineteenth century that "corrections went private," writes Friedman.[11] Public hangings became "too inflammatory" and a "new republican society had different needs and demands: self-discipline, moderation, sobriety."[12] Public humiliation simply took a different form, however, as the condemned performed manual labor in the street and on highways.[13] Offenders were no longer expected to repent or confess their sins, but the acting parts available were still limited, albeit much less gruesome and violent. All except for a particular kind of condemned, of course: American slaves. Slaves—and soon, black people in general—still deserved the whip, the lash, and the lynching tree.

For slaves in America, and then any and all black people at the turn of the nineteenth and twentieth centuries, to be black was to be condemned already to begin with. To be black was to play the role of condemned from birth forward, no crime necessary. Quoting Abdul JanMohamed, James Cone describes the black body as "'the death-bound-subject'—'the subject who is formed, from infancy on, by the imminent and ubiquitous threat of death."[14] Once threat turned to action and assault, the death-bound-subject suffered an execution as public as it was violent.

Take the case of Henry Smith, resident of Paris, Texas, in February of 1893. Smith's punishment, for having brutally raped a 4-year-old girl, provided Paris with what amounted to a state holiday and festival. "Whiskey shops were closed, unruly mobs were dispersed, schools were dismissed by a proclamation from the mayor, and everything was done in a business-like manner," writes Ida B. Wells.[15] Smith was ultimately:

> placed upon a scaffold, six feet square and ten feet high, securely bound, within full view of all beholders. Here the victim was tortured for fifty minutes by red-hot iron brands thrust against his quivering body. Commencing at the feet the brands were placed against him inch by inch until they were thrust against his face. Then, being apparently dead, kerosene was poured upon him, cottonseed hulls placed beneath him and set on fire.[16]

Little elaboration is necessary, although Wells certainly has several more examples in her reporting. Indeed, while Smith had committed an abhorrent and violent crime, black people in America, throughout the peak of its lynching years, had little more than a single part to play, regardless of how they carried themselves or what they did or did not do: that of the death-bound-subject. Little agency was afforded them, if any at all, and it is by now common knowledge that black Americans were lynched essentially for sport and spectacle, as for any other reason.

Eventually, though, as Michael Foucault writes, we come to see even "the disappearance of torture as a public spectacle."[17] But this "disappearance of public executions" and spectacle is also marked by "a slackening of the hold on the body."[18] Consequently comes a "utopia of judicial reticence: take away life, but prevent the patient from feeling it; deprive the prisoner of all rights, but do not inflict pain; impose penalties free of all pain."[19] Instead of outright, explicit, and direct punishment to the offender's body, he argues, the legal system lays claim to the offender's soul.[20] Solitary confinement, for example, is just one expression of this.

With a new focus on the soul of the condemned come new ways to deny an individual's agency. We know, however, that the bodies of the condemned—especially once incarcerated—are all too often subject to several kinds of injury, pain, and torture over extended periods of time, and for this reason, author Peter Moskos argues, of course, in defense of flogging. "If we wish to punish criminals, and we do," he writes, "flogging a man—shaming him and hurting him briefly—is better than the long-term mental torture of incarceration."[21] Though culture and society have yet to meaningfully pursue Moskos's vision, it is worth noting that were we to do so, it would much more efficiently return the condemned, the offender, to the personal and individual agency he or she enjoyed beforehand. Instead, however, we have chosen the path of mass incarceration—which is, for many of the condemned, as Michelle Alexander argues, the path of perpetual punishment.

For Alexander, the problem is as much the fact that those incarcerated are denied essential agency as it is that this denial extends beyond the correctional facility and follows the condemned far beyond their time on the inside. "Once you're labeled a felon, the old forms of discrimination— employment discrimination, housing discrimination, denial of the right to vote, denial of educational opportunity, denial of food stamps and other public benefits, and exclusion from jury service—are suddenly legal."[22] As political and social agents, certainly, those who have served time are now denied essential agency all the way through to death. "Through a web of laws, regulations, and informal rules, all of which are powerfully reinforced by social stigma, they are confined to the margins of mainstream society and denied access to the mainstream economy."[23] Such discrimination is not, technically, automatic or inevitable, but given the attitudes of this country and the larger system presently in place, it is almost ensured. This system "locks people not only behind actual bars in actual prisons, but also behind virtual bars and virtual walls—walls that are invisible to the naked eye but function nearly as effectively as Jim Crow laws once did at mocking people of color into a permanent second-class citizenship," insists Alexander.[24]

The above addresses personal, individual agency as social and political beings. In terms of the dramatic social roles played by the condemned in and for the public, the shame and stigma of being labeled a felon affects not only the offender, but "extends to family members and friends—even whole communities are stigmatized by the presence of those labeled criminals."[25] In the same way that being a black person earlier in the nineteenth century meant assuming the role of the death-bound-subject, now, argues Alexander, to be a black man "is to be thought of as a criminal, and to be a black criminal is to be despicable—a social pariah." While it may no longer be acceptable to hate black people, we are left with, and encouraged to exercise, the option to hate criminals.[26] The condemned—in this case, the black man—is not just denied a host of political and social agencies, but is also left to play the role that societal attitudes dictate: that of the social pariah.

Before I discuss the constructive possibilities of theater arts in relation to the history of punishment, denied agency, and dramatic social roles played by the condemned just discussed, I want to acknowledge the limits of theater arts in this context. While unique and meaningful—in some cases, as we will see, even life-sustaining—I admit at the outset that theater arts programs inside correctional facilities will do little to protect people who are incarcerated from all forms of violence on the inside, from all forms of labels and shame and stigma on the outside, and from a myriad of other negative, residual effects of having been identified as one of society's condemned and having served time in a correctional facility. That acknowledged, what theater arts programs can achieve especially as illustrated by the actors at MECC—is the cultivation and restoration of a multiplicity of agencies that allow the condemned to handle the above with strength, dignity, and power.

"If you don't keep exercising your mind, then you start to lose it, right?" says Brat Jones, one of the men in the production, and one of several Hamlets.[27] (Hamlet—the protagonist with more lines than any of Shakespeare's others characters—is played at MECC by four different men. "They're all on stage at the same time, taking turns delivering the lines," explains Hitt.[28]) Jones continues:

This gives me an opportunity to see a society beyond what I'm used to. I'm familiar with rap music and videos and big butts on the TV and all that. But let me come back to something that I'm not familiar with. Let me get into something else. That did open my eyes into getting into reading Sylvia Plath and Frost, and Wadsworth, and different other people.[29]

Jones is not the only one who uses the play production as an opportunity to exercise his mind and expand his intellectual and aesthetic repertoire. Timothy Lance, the only member of the cast to have done any acting previous to this production, plays the role of Osric. Osric's character is known in the theater and film world as a fop, and Lance took the liberty to research the history of fops as portrayed on stage, television, and film. "There are so many fops in television and movies," he explains to Hitt. "Nathan Lane was a little bit too much. I think Robin Williams was a little too hyper. The one that really stood out was David Hyde Pierce, his character of Niles Crane. I'd watch Frasier and kind of look at how he did things and his mannerisms. And it worked out pretty good," says Lance.[30]

Chris Harris, another of the Hamlets, has teased out several of Shakespeare's idioms and metaphors. Speaking of a moment in which Hamlet is in dialogue with Horatio, Harris says: "The sea-gown scared about me is the fog. I'm out at night. And it's the flow of the words. 'Up from my cabin, sea-gown scared about me, groped I in the dark to find out them.' Shakespeare really put some work in this. And this is the only play I've really studied from him. But he really is good."[31] Harris is one of several who can recite lines with ease from memory as he discusses his character, and the research he has done, to Hitt. Hitt notes, too, that one of the men involved in the production, through practice, rehearsal, and research, learned about himself that "he wasn't stupid, just uneducated."[32] Even Hitt learned something about the play.

"I've seen *Hamlet* a dozen times," acknowledges Hitt, including famous, productions involving Kevin Kline, Diane Venora, and Ingmar Bergman. "What else was there to learn from watching another *Hamlet?*" Hitt wondered to himself. "But the truth is, this production was different because this is a play about a man pondering a violent crime and its consequences, performed by violent criminals living out those consequences. After hanging out with this group of convicted actors for six months, I did discover something: I didn't know anything about *Hamlet*."*33*

What Hitt reveals in these instances is not just the fact that this production gave these men cause and reason to exercise their minds and intellects—to teach themselves something about literature and performing art—but that these men also had something to teach others as well. About Shakespeare, no less. And to a man who had seen the play twelve times. The guys in the play not only come into an intellectual agency, but also a pedagogical one as well. In their learning and their study, these men equip themselves to teach. Big Hutch, who plays Horatio, is another example. He stupefies Hitt for literary criticism," says Hitt. "In fact, he pointed out a weakness in the structure of the story I'd never heard before in all my experience with the play," admitted Hitt.[34]

Big Hutch illustrates another crucial example as well. His very involvement in the production precipitated an entire culture shift inside the MECC population. One of the challenges of prison theater productions, explains Hitt, is that "being a good actor is the exact emotional opposite of what it takes to be a successful inmate." While guys on the inside at MECC are all but forced to starve their capacity for sincere emotion and instead feed the pretense of affected and exaggerated strength, confidence, and prowess, in order to achieve good acting on the inside, especially, "you have to open your vulnerable self up and withstand often cruel laughter as you try to find some authentic emotion within you. In this way," says Hitt, "a level four, high-security prison is no different from high school. And so, most of the inmates who audition for Agnes tend to be 'actor-y' type people. The theater types of prison."[35] But Big Hutch, single-handedly, changed all that. His involvement with the play, given his reputation as a "blue whale" or a "killer whale" amongst all the little prison "minnows," caught the attention of the guys on the inside; it lent a kind of legitimacy to the rest of the cast, and the enterprise as a whole.[36] Big Hutch, after all, is an actor. Even killer/blue whales can be actors. This culture shift, I believe, is not unlike the kind of culture shift that successful prison theater productions can have on an audience outside the walls—a kind of socio-cultural agency, we might say.

Dennis Brown, writing for the *Riverfront Times*, a St. Louis newspaper, reviewed Act 4 after attending the performance in MECC. He called it "an astonishing success," noting that the cast "revealed itself to be as tightly disciplined, focused and motivated a unit as the St. Louis Rams."[37] The actors "rose to the challenges of this complex act," wrote Brown, and the "pace was brisk and the diction clear." One actor was described as a "commanding presence" on stage, and another as "compelling."[38] At the conclusion of the performance the actors made themselves available for a question & answer session with the audience. "When you hear an inmate speak with probing insight about Hamlet's 'intent,' you know that someone is doing something right," wrote Brown. The review concluded with a note that one of the actors was heard to have said, "This is the first time in my life anyone has ever applauded for me."[39] That Big Hutch is able to catalyze a culture shift, however slight, by his mere participation in the production of the play, it is not then impossible to imagine that successful prison theater performances and gracious, but sincere newspaper reviews of them, might catalyze a culture shift among those on the outside as well. It becomes possible for men on the inside to achieve artistic agency and identity as they create the possibility of a wider culture shift.

Back on the inside of MECC, though, the production did more than alter the prison population's attitude and social climate: it created internal communities as well. Positive ones. Constructive ones. The four men who played Hamlet are a shining example. "This small gang of Hamlets which mutters to itself and laughs at its own jokes nicely captures that fractured quality of Hamlet's different personalities," says Hitt. "And it's also bonded the four actors together. They call themselves 'the Hamlets' and constantly talk about their character."[40] Every Sunday after lunch The Hamlets met with their books and walked the prison track together, other passersby sometimes listening in as the Hamlets rehearsed and discussed their lines together. They practiced their lines every chance they got, whether they were able to assemble or not—often enough, just shouting their lines to one another from cell to cell. This image should be as powerful as any to someone thoughtful enough to relax into it and follow it to its end—the condemned, the offenders, "hardened criminals" as these people are sometimes referred to colloquially, shouting not taunts or expletives to one another, but the Early Modern English poetry and playwriting of William Shakespeare. While theater arts certainly will never substitute expletives for playwriting, shouting Shakespeare from cell to cell certainly adds a new, artistic and aesthetic vocabulary to a prison conversation.

In addition to creating community, this MECC production of Hamlet also afforded many of these men new conversations with themselves—meaningful and consequential opportunities to reflect—often in relation to the crime or crimes each of them committed. As Hitt asks Manuel Johnson, another one of the Hamlets, "When you're onstage doing Hamlet, what do you draw upon in your own experience to make the character come to life?" Johnson responds: "The idea of wanting to hurt someone. I have experienced hurting someone to the point of their life may be in danger [sic]. I was a very confused and angry person. And it escalated to me shooting two people and leaving them for dead."

Another actor, Danny Waller, chose the part he would play based on a slightly different experience with his own past. "The character I've played was the ghost of Hamlet's father. The reason I chose that, when I first read the script, the words jumped out at me. And they made me feel things that I haven't felt before," he explains. "I took a man's life. And I felt he was talking to me through that. That he wanted me to know what I put him through," explains Waller. Reciting his lines, those of King Hamlet, Waller says:

> I am thy father's spirit, doomed for a certain term to walk the night, and for the day confined to fast in fires 'til the foul crimes done in my days of nature are burnt and purged away. But that I am forbid to tell the secrets of my prison-house, I could a tale unfold whose lightest words would harrow up thy soul, freeze thy young blood and make thy two eyes, like stars, start from their spheres.

"I'm the body up there. But the words are coming from mostly William Pride, the man that I killed. He's mostly the one talking," says Waller. In this instance, in selecting the role he would play in the production, Waller actively exercised agency such that he committed himself to learning the lines of a character through which he could hear the victim of his own violent crime speaking. Waller exercised agency in a way that gave his victim voice—much like Shakespeare does with King Hamlet—and in so doing, Waller intentionally, artfully, and consequentially put himself in conversation with his victim. This role becomes a shared one, then—a role in which Waller seemingly works to reconcile himself with, or to, his victim. He exercises agency so as to give William Pride presence and voice and life from the grave.

One of Waller's fellow actors, Edgar Evans, puts himself in conversation with someone, or something, else: with God, as he understands it. Evans plays King Claudius, Hamlet's uncle. "I don't consider myself no great actor or nothing, but I try to do the best I can," he says. It was Evans's stage presence that Daniel Brown, in his Riverfront Times review, described as "commanding." Evans explains:

> And when I did the speech, I was looking upward. The chapel is at an incline there. And I was just looking up toward the top and it was like no one was there but me. I literally, honestly, didn't see a soul in the chapel when I was saying this. Maybe even—and I'm just, I'm not saying this for—it seemed almost like I was praying this actual speech to God.

Evans, a husband and father of four, feels he disappointed and failed his family by being locked up. "When I said that speech and my wife was here in the visiting room, I don't know if it had an impact on her. I don't know if she truly understood all of the content. But I wanted her to hear that speech more than anybody," he said.

Speaking of Evans' performance, even Wilcox admits the profound religiosity of the moment: "When Claudius is in the chapel and speaks about his sin and his regret and his ability to undo it, it broke my heart, because the man playing it felt all those things fully. And I know these guys have deep regrets, but it was palpable. The audience was stunned," she says.

For many, however, the chance to act—to work with others in concert, and with Agnes and her professorial colleagues—was simply a way to feel human again, to reclaim the right to feel sane and alive and human. Speaking of Agnes, Evans admits that she "makes us feel human, man. She really does. When I go in there I have to take my clothes off and get butt naked and bend over and spread my cheeks so some man can look up my butt. You know, all the humiliating things that they do to us in here. And when she comes in and does what she does," he says, "for that minute, those two and a half hours—all these guys with PhDs and could be doing other things, they come in. I at least can feel human in here."

For another, James Word, playing the role of Laertes, the play was a chance to realize a latent talent, or at least a latent aptitude—one that was clear to everybody from the start. "My wife told me that I should be an actor," he says readily. Before his incarceration Word was a con. He grew up in a neighborhood and an environment in which the good guys were the bad guys and the bad, the good. "And so, I went from this real quiet church guy to this real bad guy," he admits. "Act big, bad, tough, and I don't care, when that really wasn't me. Because when I went home at night, I felt bad about what I did. And most of the time I was scared to death doing what I was doing."

At the end of his final performance, Word knew he had done well. "And so many people were just, 'man, you were so good. Have you done this before? You should do this more. You should continue this.' And that feeling for me was just—it was one of the best feelings I've ever felt. It was like the day my daughter was born. And it made me better. Not just in acting. I mean, it just opened up a whole world for me." Even Hitt admits that Word, as an actor, "was a natural and talked about acting that way, too." In fact, Hitt insists that "Word channels Laertes' character in a way that should make any method actor cringe with jealousy."

In Word's estimation of his character's actions, he begins to provide Hitt with a way to reconcile the violent crimes these men committed with the jovial, talented actor-inmate personalities that Hitt has come to know and admire. "And [Laertes] becomes a bad guy for a little while because he's being deceitful now," Word explains. "And I can relate that to my past life as a criminal. To put a gun to somebody's face, that's an unfair advantage. And that's a cowardly act. That's what criminals are. We're cowards. When we're criminals, we are cowards." Others, like Brat Jones, admit that it has taken practice to become someone different, someone better. Danny Waller insists that "a person changes," that he is "no longer the criminal" that he once was. Having acknowledged that, even he is not sure he deserves to be on the outside. "I took a man's life. Do I deserve to be out there? I cannot say."

Prison arts programs like the one at MECC cannot, finally, answer questions like Waller's, but they can—and do—provide people who are incarcerated the chance to cultivate, reclaim, and restore multiple agencies and identities despite living within a larger system that works to deny them of all these things. The men at MECC who participated in this production achieved an intellectual and pedagogical agency and identity through rehearsing, researching, and discussing their parts. By playing against established type and reputation, actors like Big Hutch transformed the prison community's climate and culture, providing an example of what may very well be possible on a larger scale outside prison walls. The Hamlets cultivated community—to say nothing of the entire cast and their director— and many of them used the production to explore themselves, especially in relation to their victims, and, in at least one instance, even to God. These men illustrated that people can be more than the crimes they commit. In art, they realized and achieved new agency. In performance, they challenged the ultimate implications of imprisonment.

Endnotes

1. Jack Hitt, "Act V," *This American Life*, Public Radio International, WBEZ Chicago, online transcript, August 9, 2002, http://www.thisamericanlife.org/radio-archives/episode/218/transcript.
2. "Act V."
3. "Act V."
4. "Act V."
5. "Act V."
6. Lawrence M. Friedman, *Crime and Punishment in American History* (New York: Basic Books, 1993), 10.
7. Friedman, 25.
8. Friedman, 26.
9. Friedman, 37.
10. Friedman, 40.
11. Friedman, 75.
12. Friedman, 76.
13. Friedman, 78.
14. Abdul Jan Mohamed quoted in James Cone, The Cross and the Lynching Tree (Maryknoll, NY: Orbis Books, 2013), 15.
15. Ida B. Wells, "Southern Horrors: Lynch Law in All Its Phases," Southern Horrors and Other Writings: The Anti-Lynching Campaign of Ida B. Wells, 1892-1900, edited by Jacqueline Jones Royster, (Boston: Bedford/St. Martin's, 1997), 93.
16. Wells, 94.
17. Michael Foucault, Discipline & Punish: The Birth of the Prison (New York: Vintage, 1995), 7.
18. Foucault, 10.
19. Foucault, 11.
20. Foucault, 18
21. Peter Moskos, In Defense of Flogging (New York: Basic Books, 2011), 7.
22. Michelle Alexander, The New Jim Crow: Mass Incarceration in the Age of Colorblindness (New York: New Press, 2012), 2.
23. Alexander, 4.
24. Alexander, 12-3.
25. Alexander, 198.
26. Alexander, 199.
27. "Act V."
28. "Act V."
29. "Act V."
30. "Act V."

31. "Act V."
32. "Act V."
33. "Act V."
34. "Act V."
35. "Act V."
36. "Act V."
37. Daniel Brown, "Captive Audience," Riverfront Times (St. Louis, MO), Feb. 6, 2002.
38. Brown, "Captive Audience."
39. Brown, "Captive Audience."
40. "Act V."
41. "Act V."
42. "Act V."
43. "Act V."
44. "Act V."
45. "Act V."
46. "Act V."
47. "Act V."
48. "Act V."
49. "Act V."
50. "Act V."
51. "Act V."
52. "Act V."
53. "Act V."
54. "Act V."

Bibliography

Alexander, Michelle. *The New Jim Crow: Mass Incarceration in the Age of Colorblindness*. New York: New Press, 2012.

Brown, Daniel. "Captive Audience." *Riverfront Times* (St. Louis, MO), Feb. 6, 2002.

Cone, James. *The Cross and the Lynching Tree*. Maryknoll, NY: Orbis Books, 2013.

Foucault, Michael. Discipline & Punish: The Birth of the Prison. New York: Vintage, 1995.

Friedman, Lawrence M. *Crime and Punishment in American History*. New York: Basic Books, 1993.

Hitt, Jack. "Act V." *This American Life*. Public Radio International & WBEZ Chicago.

Online transcript. August 9, 2002
http://www.thisamericanlife.org/radioarchives/episode/218/ transcript.

Moskos, Peter. *In Defense of Flogging*. New York: Basic Books, 2011.

Wells, Ida B. *Southern Horrors and Other Writings: The Anti-Lynching Campaign of Ida B. Wells, 1892-1900*. Boston: Bedford/St. Martin's, 1993.

Overcoming Recidivism from A Position Of Inequality

Mark D. Brouillard

"Prison Based Education Is The Single Most
Effective Tool For Lowering Recidivism"
-U.S. Department of Justice

Abstract

The United States incarcerates more people than any other nation in the free world today (Wright,2010,p.1). For well over two decades, our nation's political and criminal justice policy makers have pursued unsuccessful, tough-on-crime policies that have completely failed to address the real causes of crime, such as homelessness, unemployment, drug addiction, mental illness, and illiteracy, among many others. In fact, from the beginning of prisons to today's prison crisis of mass incarceration,[1] prison administrators are focused on rehabilitating the moral (ethical) character of an individual through manual labor, isolation, and corporal punishment (Friedman,193). All the while, our country's policy makers have intentionally failed to address the real problem: lack of education among citizens re-entering society from prisons. This catastrophic failure has served to maintain a "system of wealth" that has produced over "six million people" who are either incarcerated or are under some sort of "correctional supervision," in other words, one out of every one hundred Americans is serving time behind bars (Taylor,2001,p.49 Whithead,2012,p.1). Although these citizens come from all walks of life, most are poor, uneducated, black or latino, considered members of the lower class and therefore, "outcasts not wanted in today's society" (Taylor,2001,22).

Introduction

By removing what political and criminal justice policy makers consider "social junk", an unequal distribution of power and wealth is created, one that leaves both the poor and people with criminal records (who have served their time) in an insurmountable struggle for survival (Taylor,2001., p.61). As a consequence, many citizens released from prison return to those habituated behaviors that had sent them to prison in the first place, in order to provide for their loved ones. This paper examines how post-secondary education enables a convicted criminal to overcome the social injustices that are inherent in a class-based bureaucratic system.

Part I highlights a brief history of the image of crime and how it works to create an inequality that keeps the rich powerful and the poor disenfranchised through a terrorizing system of social fear. Part II shows how political and criminal justice leaders have intentionally dropped the ball by excluding post-secondary education as moral rehabilitation, while skillfully weaving the prison system into our country's social fabric. Part III reveals, how the intentional othering by political and criminal justice policy makers serves to marginalize the poor, lower class, and recently released uneducated citizens, essentially keeping them uneducated, unemployable, and homeless. Instead of teaching prisoners the real skills of "The moral life of downtown; the humanities, the study of' human conducts and concerns; in order to eliminate the distinction between the rich and the poor, policy makers have opted to "exploit social and natural circumstances to their own advantage" claims Rawls (Shorris,1997,p.3, 13, 75-83). In conjunction with Part III, Part IV illustrates the social injustices and obstacles that returning citizen's face, which prohibit a successful transition back to society. As an example, returning citizens are allowed to be discriminated against for housing, employment, and certain educational opportunities. Moreover, there are very strict policies in effect, such as probation and parole fees, child support, and court fines, that work to enhance recidivism. All of these issues serve to prevent any type of upward mobility for people with criminal records.

However, as I contend in Parts V through VII, post-secondary education, such as the Boston University Prison Education Program (P.E.P.), paralegal degree programs, or any other type of accredited degree program offered to prisoners, all work to enhance successful re-entry for returning citizens. Part V details programs of post secondary education that equip citizens for re-entry. Part VI compares rates of recidivism for those returning to society without higher education versus those with higher education. Part VIII argues for those specific skills developed in post-secondary education that result in a returning citizen avoiding recidivism.

Before presenting my argument, I would like to disclose how the Boston University P.E.P. program has transformed my life from what Mark Lewis Taylor argues, as "other...whom a society's policy makers often see as expendable" to a man of intellectual value and moral integrity who is considered a socially acceptable individual and is worthy of redemption

(Taylor,2001,p.49). First, the B.U.P.E.P. has taught me how to think critically, not only about worldly issues, but it has given me the skills necessary to overcome issues that have served to cause my incarceration e.g. anger, racism, violence, and a know-everything attitude that was quickly humbled after I realized the vast array of knowledge available in the B.U. Prison Education Program. Boston University has prepared me to fight what Earl Shorris terms the "surround of force, which is what keeps the poor from being political, and that for absence of politics in their lives was what kept them poor. I don't mean "political' in the sense of voting in an election but in the way Thucydides used the word: to mean activity with other people at every level, from the family to the neighborhood to the broader concept to the broader community to the city-state" (1997,p.1). Earl Shorris's ingenious concept is what got me through the interview process and accepted into the B.U. P.E.P. program. In which, are acquired the "political" skills needed to face society head on and succeed. Hence, the true premise of this literary work, which is my own experience of a post-secondary educational transformation during my fifteen years in prison to something more than what society considers "a disease" (Friedman, 1993,p.15).

Overcoming Recidivism from a Position Of Inequality

Image Of Crime And Its Purpose: Social Control Through Fear

When one thinks of crime, most people think of violent acts like robbery, murder, or rape, which are supposedly committed by a person who comes from a lower income neighborhood or is black, because a person who is rich or from the upper class could not possibly commit lower class acts like rape or murder. In the words of Richard Snyder, "The classifications of people of color as inferior and of criminals as garbage to be thrown away have combined to foster a response to crime that is basically one of vengeance and punishment" (2001,p.54). Crime is associated with blacks and criminals in this manner because society's view of crime has been intentionally distorted by both the media and policy makers, who have created an animalistic lower class image of crime in order to keep society in a state of perpetual fear for their own financial gain. Mark Lewis Taylor insists that this creates "economic disparity, which has called forth its necessary compliment, a terrorizing system of military application of force (as in Iraq) and the punitive regime of Gulag America" (2001,p.54). Because policy makers are in a position of power that influence the lives of every citizen of the country, their statements have a major impact on how we understand the law and its effect on crime. When our leaders decide what is a crime, who is a criminal, and most importantly, where these people come from, one could say that crime itself is created.

It is common to see politicians who are running for political office talking about crime and making commitments to pass bills to prevent violent crime and "protect" the public. By targeting the criminal element of our society, and focusing on cleaning up the communities of color, immigrants, the unemployed, homeless, and those who have a diminishing claim to social resources, both policy makers and the media produce images the public will be able to associate with criminal behavior (Davis,1998,p.97).

What is really happening is the intentional formation of a terrorizing fear that produces social control over the disenfranchised underclass, which is reinforcing inequality in our society. During his 1994 State of The Union Address, President Clinton used this exact form of terrorizing fear on crime tactic by comparing criminals in the United States to terrorist actions against the U.S. from foreign countries. Clinton claimed, "violent crime and the fear it provokes leaves us less secure at home than we, are from threats abroad" (Reiman,2007,p.12). This tough-on-crime stance was viewed as a positive step in reducing crime, but this was not the case. What it really did was launch the largest prison project in the nation's history, diverting money from education, employment, and other agencies to fund the expansion of prisons (Western,2008, p.4). There was absolutely no mention of crime prevention, the rehabilitation or treatment of criminal offenders, or any plan to reintegrate the thousands of people released yearly from prisons back into society, Cinton's address was just another tough-on-crime policy that offered no real solutions, but only served to support the greedy intentions of political and criminal justice policy makers.

II

Missing the Mark: Policy Makers Intentions

In the early 1830s, there were two institutions in the United States that were considered to be leading examples of how to manage criminals. They were Auburn State Prison in New York and the Eastern Penitentiary in Philadelphia. These institutions focused on correcting the morals of an individual through rigorous programs of work and isolation (Western,2005,p.2). At the time, this new system was billed as a triumph of progressive thinking, one that supposedly provided a humane and rational alternative to the disorderly prisons and houses of corrections in Europe (Western,2005,pgs.1,2). In practice, this process combined isolation, corporal punishment, and correcting one's moral direction in order to re-establish the offender as a functioning member of society. Along with the concept of prisons sat an array of other welfare institutions, including reformatories, asylums, public schools, and hospitals that were allegedly designed to help those who had fallen into poverty and crime (Western,2005,pgs.1,2).

However, somewhere along the way, the process of rehabilitation was lost and by the late nineteen-seventies, most political and local leaders had become skeptical that prisons could prevent crime and rehabilitate the inmates in them. Incarceration would now be employed as a deterrent, an instrument of punishment and not rehabilitation (Western, 2005,pgs.1,2). It is at this juncture, where policy makers began missing their mark. Instead of focusing on a human being's intellectual value, they began to hone in on more aggressive punishment methods, such as solitary confinement, which has been proven to induce psychological behavior problems. Thus, instead of changing an inmate's behavior for the better, they made one twice as likely to commit acts of violence against staff and/or other inmates upon one's release from solitary confinement. To illustrate that from the perspective of a prisoner of fifteen years, inmates are forced to adapt to a prison environment, within which they forget how to socialize normally. There becomes an atmosphere of aggressive tension that is created between the prison guards and their captives, because most Department of Correction employees develop an attitude that prisoners are to be treated as animals and continually punished. On the opposite side, prisoners feel that their punishment is the loss of their freedom, hence, their punishment is their prison term itself and the prison guards do not have the right to continuously act abusivly. As a result, the prisoner loses his true identity and any signs of docility by adopting a tough-guy persona, even if he is not. The reason for this is because a weak character in prison is a sign of a weak individual. In prison, kindness is often mistaken for weakness, so prisoners are always vigilant of other prisoners acts of kindness; to the point that a paranoia develops which, in turn, produces an animosity among the prisoners themselves that often results in violence.

As if that were not enough stress on one's psychological welfare; prisoners have their own internal hierarchy that judges each individual upon his or her crime. At the top of the prison food chain sits the murderers, at the bottom are the child molesters. So, as an example, let us view the concerns for the moral rehabilitation of an individual on the bottom of the prison food chain. Moral rehabilitation becomes secondary to an individual caught up in this overtly precarious position. In fact, the post-secondary education that is necessary for intellectual value and reshaping of one's moral character become the furthest thing from one's mind in this position. In a punitive tough guy prison culture, inmates are too busy trying to act bad as a means of trying to earn respect that they completely lose their identity and forget that re-educating oneself is the only answer to one not returning to prison.

By policy makers creating a punitive dog-eat-dog prison environment, prisoners are constantly enclosed in a pressure cooker of aggressive behavior, which manifests itself into non-social behavior. This, in turn, affects society as a whole when a prisoner is released to the street with this untreated pent-up internal anger. As a consequence of internalizing volatile emotions over long periods of time, an inmate often becomes institutionalized and he begins to identify with his oppressor. That is, he loses his identity, forgets; how to act and succumbs to being abused with an air that the abuse is natural and he deserves to be treated this way. So, upon release from confinement, an institutionalized prisoner is not prepared to deal with the obstacles he must face, like finding employment. Thus, when trying to transition back to society and regain one's identity one has a difficult time acting autonomously and so they revert back to criminal behavior in order to survive.

However, prisoners have a saying behind these walls of desolation and despair. "You can let the time do you, or you can do the time." As a prisoner, one realizes there are only two ways to survive a prison sentence, you can fight and rebel (continuing the behavior that brought you to prison), or you can reorient your priorities and take advantage of the time in order to educate yourself through submersing yourself in the humanities. Even though policy makers have intentionally dropped the ball by getting tough on crime in lieu of focusing on education, that does not excuse a prisoner's choice to not be smart and change his future.

The politicians vowed to get tough on crime, and they did, by weaving their necessity for prisons agenda into our social fabric. Federal and state lawmakers abandoned any rehabilitative ideals and opted for a more draconian approach by getting "tough on crime" creating mandatory minimum sentences and truth in sentencing, which added longer sentences for second and third time offenders, and placed limitations on parole (Western ,2002~p.2,3). Over the decades, this tough on crime mentality has produced a mass incarceration to the point where prisons across the United States are overcrowded and are at their breaking point with both the number of prisoners they hold and the rising costs to house and care for them. Angela Davis recently stated, "Short of major wars, mass incarceration has been the most thoroughly implemented government social program of our time" (Davis,1998,p.3).

Sadly, the United States is number one in incarcerating its citzens. Presently, over seven million U.S. citizens are under some form of correctional care, custody, or control. Not only do we imprison more of our citizens than any other country in the world, the numbers are not even close. China is second with one point five million of its citizens behind bars (however, it is first in executing its citizens), and Russia is a distant third with eight hundred and ninety thousand inmates (Warren, 2008 ,pgs.2,3, Waldman,2013 ,pgs.1-8) Massachusetts is very much. a part of this incarceration problem with an estimated 11,000 inmates as of January 1, 2013, at a cost of $6 billion annually to house and care for these inmates (Mass Inc.,2013,p.18, MA DOC Inmate Statistics,2013,p.7). As of mid-year 2004, 1 in 24 adults in Massachusetts was under some form of correctional care, custody, or control (PEW,2006,p.1). Since 1990, new commitments to Massachusetts DOC prisons have increased by one third (Mass Inc., p.12). With an overall projected increase to over 13,000 inmates by 2018, policy makers will be forced to start re-thinking their counter-productive tough on crime policies (MA DOC Strategic Plan, 2010-2015,p.8). As a consequence of policy makers across the nation weaving mass incarceration into our social fabric, thirteen million people are introduced to American jails in any given year. The benefit of increased mass incarceration for our political leaders and policy makers is clear: more prisons equals more profits (Whitehead, 2012,pgs.1,2).

III

A Class-Based Bureaucratic System

Political actions that are supportive of a system of bureaucratic social control have been the cause of numerous race; poverty, crime, and class-based social problems throughout history. For example, Michelle Alexander, in her book The New Jim Crow, compares the political stance of the war on drugs to the new form of Jim Crow laws that serve to segregate people of color through racial and class based discrimination that drives the criminal justice system (Alexander, 2010). It is this type of class-based, intention other intentional othering that political and criminal justice policy makers use to marginalize the poor, lower class, and recently-released, uneducated ex-prisoners to enhance their "system of wealth" and power (Taylor.,2001,p.22). Jeffrey Reiman contends, "that our outrageous criminal justice policies and practices are actually a well planned strategy" 2007,p.47). A strategy he terms the "Pyrrhic Defeat" theory, which states, the war on crime is a failure and an avoidable one at that. Our criminal justice policy creates the "reality" of crime as the work of the. poor and people of color, projecting an image that disenfranchises this lower class in order to serve the rich and powerful (Reiman,2007,. pgs.47,49).

Supporting his theory, Reiman uses the work of Michael Foucault, who also suggests that the failure of the criminal justice system prisons in particular serves a function in society, that this class-based explanation of the new prison regime in which criminality gets identified almost exclusively [with] a certain social class the bottom rank of the social order (Reiman ,2007',pgs.47,48). This is where I believe the work of John Rawls becomes important. In his book, A Theory of Justice, Rawls argues for economic justice through a theory he terms the "difference principle." The difference principle occurs when economic inequalities are unjust unless they work to maximize the share of the worst off group in society, by providing incentives that increase production over all. This implies that inequalities are only just if they reduce the share of the worst off group (Reiman,2007,p.31). For example, since most of the rich and powerful come from the upper class and have the educational requirements and economic resources to run for elected office, they are already groomed for success, hence the "difference principle" Rawls suggests. This type of advantage does not serve to increase overall production; rather, it serves to keep certain individuals in power who then serve the interests of a particular group. In fact, the upper class are most likely to become lawmakers themselves and work to make laws that further suppress the lower-class. Above all, the decisions they make only serve to increase the stratification of our society and serve to support Reiman's theory that the system, by design, is a failure. However, this failure can be prevented by reforming those current laws that govern sentencing, the prison system, and education.

IV

Social Injustices: Obstacles Returning Prisoners Face

After decades of failed "tough on crime" policies that have resulted in prison overcrowding to the point of double-bunking maximum security facilities, such as Souza-Baranowski in Shirley, Massachusetts, something has to be done in order to reverse the popular trend of warehousing inmates for profit. What our political leaders need to do is address some of the obstacles that returning citizens face in order to avoid recidivism; these include; discrimination for housing, employment, educational opportunities, and a variety of strict policies that work to enhance recidivism. Such policies include probation and parole fees, child support, and court fees all of which inhibit upward mobility and keep former prisoners caught in a vicious cycle of recidivism. The criminal justice system will continue to fail and returning citizens will continue to face obstacles that are virtually impossible to overcome unless there is a complete overhaul of our justice system.

What our political leaders need to do is conduct a comprehensive review of the laws governing sentencing guidelines, the re-entry process, and the availability of higher education for inmates. Any inmate released from prison should have a clean slate that precludes any and all probation, parole, medical, and housing fees. In this way, they will be afforded a chance at surviving prison release in an obstacle-free manner. Our political leaders need to have the "will" to take a stand and be "smart on crime" instead of being seen as tough on crime, because their policies are not working. Our political leaders are well aware that it takes a college education or technical training to survive in today's world.

Equally important is the fact that approximately 94% of the Massachusetts state prison population will be released back into society unequipped to faces any obstacles due to their lack of education or life skills necessary to succeed in life or society (Reiman, 2007, pgs.97,167-171). Presently, 60% of all offenders in the system read below the ninth grade level and 56% of male, 40% of female, offenders enter the system with less than a sixth grade level in math proficiency (MA DOC Strategic Plan 2010-2015,p.4). With statistics like these it is apparent why there is a need for higher, or post-secondary, education.

With more than 700,000 inmates being released from prisons yearly across the United States, local and state officials are beginning to search for effective methods to help these men and women successfully re-integrate back into society (Contardo & Tolbert, 2013, p.1.) A primary example of this is a program called Ready 4 Reentry, a prisoner reentry toolkit for faith-based and community organizations, which is sponsored by the United States Department of Labor. This sixty-five page comprehensive reentry package features innovative practices, job descriptions, and various documents from the Ready 4 Work Prisoner Reentry Demonstration. This program helps a returning citizen remove barriers to employment and has shown that, when compared against the recidivism benchmark from the Bureau of Justice Statistics (BJS) re-incarceration study, "Recidivism of Prisoners Released in 1994," R4W recidivism rates are half the national reincarceration rate of 5% at six months and 44% lower than the 10.4% national rate of incarceration one-year after release (U.S. Department of Labor, p.3). With this one educational re-entry work tool kit, R4W placed 2,543 participants (57%) into jobs, with 63% of those placed retaining their jobs for three consecutive months after placement. On average, program costs were approximately $4,500 per participant, compared with average costs of $25,000 to $40,000 per year for re-incarceration. With statistics like this, our political and criminal justice leaders would have to be blind not to see that education is the key to success (U.S. Dept of Labor RW4 tool kit).

V

Post-secondary Education: Preparing Citizens for Re-entry

Despite the obstacles that recently released citizens face upon their return to society, there is a possible solution to recidivism for those who truly want to transform their lives: Post-secondary education while incarcerated (Contardo & Tolbert 2013 ,p.1). Post-secondary education is any education or academic course taken for college credit that occurs after one has already obtained a high school diploma or high school equivalency (GED). One of the most readily available examples of higher education is that provided by community colleges, which have a century-old-tradition of expanding educational access to everyone, including inmates (Contardo & Tolbert, 2013 p.3). In a recent IHEP study, it was found that 68% of all post-secondary correctional education is provided by community colleges. The fact that community colleges tend to cost less, have a greater flexibility in courses, and are supported from the local community and industrial populations, makes them a perfect fit for the correctional setting (Contardo & Tolbert,2013,p.3).

On the same side, there is currently a four-year (post-secondary) liberal arts degree offered by Boston University's PEP, whose purpose is to equip returning citizens with those skills necessary for a successful re-entry. This program works to transform one's character, intellectual value, and moral virtue. Aristotle argues, that there are "two kinds of virtues; intellectual and moral, intellectual virtue in the main owes both its birth and its growth to teaching (for which reason requires experience and time), while moral virtue comes as a result of habit" (Singer/Aristotle, no date;p.26). If moral virtue is habit while intellectual virtue is taught, and neither comes naturally, and we adhere to Aristotle's theory that "nothing that exists by nature can form a habit contrary to its nature" (Singer/Aristotle no date,p.26), then we must consider if virtues are habit forming, then we are the only ones who can re-orient our lives in order to re-educate ourselves. The Boston University Prison Education Program gives one the opportunity to earn a college degree while transforming one's life through an education in the humanities. Every prisoner holds the potential to exhibit good behavior. However, one must first acknowledge his or her potentiality, and act upon this realization, in order to change their bad behavior. Aristotle claimed that "states of character arise out of like activities. This is why the activities we exhibit must be of a certain kind; it is because This the states of character correspond to the differences between these. It makes no small difference, then, whether we form habits of one kind or another from our very youth, it makes a great difference, or rather all the difference" (Singer, no date,p.26).

Boston University's post-secondary prison program not only helps prisoners equip themselves for re-entry into society, but it enhances their intellectual value and transforms their moral being. Most prisoners have developed abnormal, socially unacceptable behavior since their youth. Post secondary education gives every individual who participates in it the opportunity to transpose those ingrained habits. Thus, one develops socially-acceptable habits that help them avoid recidivism.

VI

Recidivism Rate: Without and With Higher Education

James Forman Jr. asserts, "there is a close connection between incarceration rates and educational attainment: Blacks and Whites who have dropped out of high school are ten times more likely to recidivate than those who have attended college" (2012,p.143). Most prisoners are uneducated, have mental health issues, and, more often than not, are released without treating any of these issues. Hence, most returning citizens find they do not have the necessary education to overcome the forces of social control, keeping them from ever attaining higher education, which heaps "additional disabilities upon existing disadvantage" (Forman, 2012,pgs.101-10:5) However statistics clearly show that, by having a post-secondary degree, rates of recidivism are drastically reduced:

1. A three state recidivism study made in 1997 by Steurer, Smith, and Tracy showed that inmates who participated in higher education programs while in prison reduced their re-incarceration rate by 29% (2001,p.1).

2. According to the National Correctional Association's 2009 report, inmates who earned an AA/AS degree are 70% less likely to recidivate than those who do not complete a program (Esperien,2010,p.32).

3. A recent U.S. Department of Justice report claims that "Prison-based education is the single most effective tool for lowering recidivism." The exact figures detailing these inverse recidivism rates for degree recipients were as follows: Associates 13.7%; Bachelors 5.6%; Masters 0% (Esperien,2010,p.324)

As more and more information becomes available, the picture becomes clearer for all those who choose to see it. Post-secondary education is the answer for a returning citizen's successful re-integration to society. The claim that higher education reduces recidivism is supported by the Boston University Prison Education Program, which offers prisoners a four-year degree in Liberal Arts.(the humanities). Recidivism rates for this program are currently estimated at 1% (statistic acquired through the B. U. clerk); there are tangible benefits from this degree. At a recent educational seminar held at MCI-Norfolk state prison, one job specialist indicated that he had a 100% placement rate for inmates leaving prison with a bachelors degree. The representative went on to state that the B.U. degree prevails over the effects of Criminal Offender Record Information check and that many employers are willing to "leave the past in the past." Statistics clearly demonstrate that post-secondary education helps to deter recidivism and to this end, it undoubtedly prepares one with the skills for a successful transition from prison back into society.

Specific Skills Developed from Post-secondary Education Post-secondary education equips returning citizens with the skills to overcome the

> "numerous forces-hunger, isolation, illness, landlords, police, abuse, neighbors, drugs, criminals, racism, among many others ... [which] ... exert themselves on the poor at all times and enclose them, making up a 'surround of force' from which, it seems, they cannot escape" (Shorris, 1997,p.1).

As discussed in Parts I through IV, political and criminal policy makers have carefully woven the prison system into our social fabric by creating this "surround of force" that Earl Shorris speaks of (1997,p.1). They have created an unequal, unjust obstacle course through a terrorizing system of social fear and intentional othering that serves to marginalize the poor. This system of terror assists policy makers in creating their reality of crime, which keeps society in a constant state of fear in order to maintain their system of wealth, power, and social control over the poor. As a result, a returning citizen must equip him nor herself with the skills to over come this intentional othering by society. Post-secondary education arms one with specific skills to overcome the intentional membership of the stigmatized caste system, which has condemned them to a life time of second-class citizenship (Forman,2012,p.110).

What an inmate encounters during the transition back into the community and how well he is equipped and supported in handling that process is key to a successful transition. An important skill that is acquired through post-secondary education is how to deal with any and all "political" situations, especially overcoming the intentional othering inflicted by policy makers. Earl Shorris believes, "that this is what kept the poor from being political and that the absence of politics in their lives was what kept them poor. I don't mean 'political' in the sense of voting in an election, but in the way Thucydides used the word: to mean activity with people at every level, from the family to the neighborhood to the broader community to the city-state" (1997,p.1). Higher education provides a returning citizen with the social skill needed to succeed in any situation.

By studying the constructs of human concerns, one is able to conquer the separation and removal from society and the less than status which keeps us from conducting ourselves like conscious adults. Hiding one's shame behind a constant, inhumane othering induces a predictable outcome: violent criminal activity. However, higher education gives one the skill to push past "second class citizenship" (Forman,2012,p.110).

By studying the humanities, one gains numerous transitional skills that help them re-enter society with a structural system of knowledge and social well-being. For example:

1. Collaboration skills--these skills are valuable when dealing with supervisory agencies such as Parole and Probation.

2. Extensive writing skills--writing and other forms of communications skills necessary for addressing legal matters; a socially acceptable way to argue a point with various social agencies among other obstacles.

3. Organizational skills--these skills help to keep one from missing probation appointments, help with financial and business matters, and generally help guide one through a successful transition.

4. Development of social skills the humanities taught in higher education gives one the opportunity to open one's mind to social settings that they may have never even contemplated. The opportunity to see from another's point of view opens one up to a whole new world.

5. Responsibility--accepting responsibility is a skill--that most prisoners lack. When one takes the opportunity to contemplate the responsibility of their actions and their consequences through ethics, a certain drive develops with the attainment of intellectual value and moral virtue, which completely alters one's being.

6. Skills to market oneself properly-skills that allow one to enter and remain in the workplace (resume, public speaking, presentation skills, self-promoting, etc.).

These skills are among the many gained by higher education that help one learn how to navigate the social and political life that Earl Sharris believes is the way out of poverty. Having been in prison for the past fifteen years myself, and experiencing the powers of the surround of force Sharris speaks of, I can attest that post-secondary education is the only avenue to gain those skills necessary to provide an entrance to the political life. The poor and incarcerated do not need anyone to release them; an escape route exists. However, in order for a returning citizen to be successful upon re-entry, he or she must first garner the social skills through post-secondary education to overcome any and all obstacles that they will face upon release. Through education, the major distinction between the life of the rich and the life of the poor is eliminated (Sharris,1997,p.3).

VIII

Conclusion

An individual's release from prison without post-secondary education is effectively a guaranteed return trip back. The government has placed far too many obstacles in a returning citizen's path, making it virtually impossible for a former prisoner to overcome poverty and truly turn away from their criminal past in order to become a law abiding citizen. However, post-secondary education gives one the skills and opportunity to function in social situations on the same level as those who create the laws that decide who is socially acceptable.

Our society demands fair and just sentences that work to maintain public safety, punish properly, and attempt to reform criminal behavior. With that said, post-secondary education, as taught by the humanities gives a prisoner, who is accustomed to habituated criminal behavior, the rare opportunity to contemplate his or her unlawful behavioral issues, which have been ingrained in them since their youth. More importantly, it presents an individual with the option to gain intellectual value and moral virtue through critical thinking. As a result, a prisoner acquires the skills necessary to navigate the world of social politics and overcome it. Moreover, by transforming their moral character to a level that society considers securely reformed and once again acceptable, a recently released prisoner can be safely returned to the community.

Endnotes

1 Mass incarceration on a scale almost unexampled in human history is a fundamental fact of our country today – perhaps the fundamental fact, as slavery was the fundamental fact of 1850. In truth, there are more black men in the grip of the criminal justice system – in prison, on probation, or on parole – than were in slavery the. Overall, there are now more people under 'correctional supervision' in America – more than six million – than were in Gulag Archipelago under Stalin at its height. The Caging of America, as cited in (Whitehead, 2012, p.1)

Works Cited

Alexander, Michelle. 2012. The New Jim Crow: Mass Incarceration in the Age of Colorblindeness. New Press Publishing.

Contardo, Jeanne, Tolbert, Michelle. 2013. "Prison Post-secondary Education:" Bridging Learning From Incarceration to the Community. Retrieved February 6, 2014.

Davis, Angela. 1998. "Masked Racism:" Reflections on the Prison Industrial Complex. The World Traveler (Fall).

Esperian, John. 2010. "The Effect of Prison Education Progra.ms on Recidivism." The Journal of Correctional Education 61(4).

Forman, Ben, Larivee, John. 2013. "Crime, Cost, and Consequences:" Is It Time to Get Smart on Crime. Mass Inc.

Forman, Jr., James. 2012 "Racial Critiques of Mass Incarceration:" Beyond the New Jim Crow. Racial Critiques.

Friedman, Lawrence. 1993. Crime and Punishment in American History. New York, NY: Basic Books.

Massachusetts Department of Corrections. 2010. Strategic Plan 2010-2015. Retrieved February 6, 2014.http://www.Mass.gov.

PEW. 2006. Massachusetts. 1 in 31 The Long Reach of American Corrections. Retrieved Febraury 6, 2014. www.pewcenteronthe states.org.

Rawls, John. 1971. A Theory of Justice. Boston, MA: The Belknap Press of Harvard University Press Cambridge.

Ready 4 Reentry. (no date). Prisoner Tool Kit For Faith Based and Community Organizations.

Reiman, Jeffrey. 2007. The Rich Get Richer and the Poor Get Prison.: Ideology, Class and Criminal Justice. Boston, MA: Pearson.

Shorris, Earl. 1997. As a Weapon in the hands of the restless poor. Harpers Magazine (Fall).

Singer, Peter. (no date). Ethics. Oxford Paperbacks. Oxford University Press.

Works Cited

Snyder, Richard. 2001. The Protestant Ethic and the Spirit of Punishment. William B. Publishing Co. Grand Rapids, MI.

Steur, Steven, Smith, Linda, Tracy, Alice. 2001. OCE/OEA Three state Recidivism Study. Correctional Education Association, Lanham, MD.

Taylor, Mark. 2001. The Executed God: The Way of the Cross in Lockdown America. Minneapolis, MN: Fortress press.

Waldman, Paul. 2013. Six Charts that Explain Why Our Prison System Is So Insane. Retrieved February 6, 2014.http://prospect.org.

Warren, Jennifer. 2008. One in 100: Behind Bars in America 2008. Washington DC: PEW Charitable Trust.

Western, Bruce. 2005. Introduction. Punishment and Inequality in America. (handout) 2013. The Prison Problem. Harvard Magazine. Retrieved February 6, 2014. http://harvardmagazine.com.

Whitehood, John. 2-012. Jailing Americans for Profit: The Rise of the Prison Industrial Complex. Retrieved February 6, 2014. http://www.ratherford.org.

Wright, Walerie. 2010. Deference in Criminal Justice. Evaluating Certainty Vs. Severity of Punishment. The Sentencing Project.

www.ingramcontent.com/pod-product-compliance
Lightning Source LLC
Chambersburg PA
CBHW031837170526
45157CB00001B/333